What People Are S~~~~
James W. Goll and Th~~~~

When I think about my friend James Goll, I think of a man without compromise, a man without guile. He reminds me of the prophet Daniel in the Scriptures because he is single in focus and a man of integrity. His life, in good times and in bad, seems to be a prophetic parable of God's limitless grace working in the life of His servant. This servant of the Lord is also one of the finest students of the Word I have ever met. His pursuit of all that is true seems to attract insights and revelation in a measure that is not normal for most of us. James Goll's passion is to make it practical, and then give it all away. I believe the book *The Discerner* is a gift from this prophet to the church. And much like his book *The Seer*, it will mark the church for decades to come. Read, enjoy, and be inspired, equipped, and empowered *for such a time as this.*

—Bill Johnson
Bethel Church, Redding, CA
Author, *When Heaven Invades Earth* and *God Is Good*

As I travel the nation teaching spiritual warfare principles, one truth becomes painfully clear: the body of Christ, at large, lacks discernment. The reality is that many believers have simply not been activated or trained to discern spirits. Yet discernment is a vital gift in this hour as false prophets, false teachers, and even false christs are rising around the world with smooth sayings, rhymes, and riddles.

Discerning of spirits is one of the nine gifts of the Holy Spirit Paul lists in 1 Corinthians 12:7–11. It is the Holy Spirit-inspired ability to distinguish between the operations of the Holy Spirit, a demon spirit, and the human spirit. Discerning of spirits is especially helpful in prophecy, where we need to test the spirits to see if they are of God (1 John 4:1). It's also vital in spiritual warfare so that we accurately determine what we're battling instead of just beating the air through guessing games (1 Corinthians 9:26).

James Goll's latest book, *The Discerner*, equips the body in discernment. Given the goings-on in the world and in the church, this book is right on time. Readers will understand, with clarity, how to press in to the gift of discernment in its many manifestations, as well as cultivate biblical discernment to test the spirits. I thank God that James wrote this practical book. It is truly for such a time as this.

—*Jennifer LeClaire*
Senior Editor, *Charisma* and *SpiritLed Woman*
Senior Leader, Awakening House of Prayer, Fort Lauderdale, FL

I admire Prophet James Goll for the tremendous influence he has been for so many years, and continues to be, in the prophetic awakening in the body of Christ. I consider him to be one of the end-time prophets who not only accurately prophesies the future but also brings a powerful manifestation of worship and miracles in the now whenever he flows in the prophetic. He is a seasoned man of the Word who knows how to hear the voice of the Spirit of God so as to bring a fresh revelation and to teach others how to apply what the Spirit is saying to the church today.

His latest book, *The Discerner*, carries important truth and revelation the church desperately needs: to detect and defeat the deception of the spirit of this age, we must tune in to discern and hear the voice of truth from our Shepherd, Jesus. I recommend *The Discerner*, as it will help readers understand how to cultivate a greater level of biblical discernment in general, as well as how to activate and grow in the gift of discernment in particular. Full of deep yet palatable revelation and practical teaching, I am sure that this book will serve countless believers as a beacon in the dark and as a compass accurately pointing northward.

—*Apostle Guillermo Maldonado*
King Jesus International Ministry, Miami, FL

I have known James Goll for over a decade. My friend and, even more, this friend of God, is known for combining three strands of truth together in whatever he does. James brings a weight of scriptural teaching to produce a solid foundation. He then builds upon this by adding a second component of precedents found in Jewish and church history. This is followed by a third necessary ingredient of contemporary testimonies of the work of the Holy Spirit today. James has done it for us once again in *The Discerner*. What an excellent handbook to help believers in Messiah know how to live a supernatural life with effectiveness today.

—*Sid Roth*
Host, *It's Supernatural!* TV
Author, evangelist, and inspirational speaker

I just finished reading James Goll's new book, *The Discerner*, and—wow! Let me say it this way: there are many books about hearing God's voice, but this goes way deeper, gifting you from the riches of James's life experience and prophetic ministry. It gives you a road map for navigating how to manifest the revelation you receive, and letting God change your very nature in the process. James is an encyclopedia of revelation and supernatural materials, and this book is like a capstone of all his previous wonderful works on revelatory gifting. I highly recommend it, and I immensely enjoyed it!

—*Shawn Bolz*
www.bolzministries.com

It would be difficult to imagine a time in which discernment was more important than now. James Goll has been an observer of, participant in, or leader of almost every important wave of the Holy Spirit in ministry for forty years and is perfectly suited to teach the church how to navigate the various competing moral, spiritual, and political paradigms in this modern world. His new book, *The Discerner*, is full of rich insight and allows us to benefit from all that experience as he has watched and interacted with leaders, churches, denominations, and movements. As you meditate on this book, you will gain a greater understanding of the forces that affect your life and how to intelligently maintain your walk with God. Read, learn, and grow up in Christ.

—*Joan Hunter*
Author and Healing Evangelist
Joan Hunter Ministries

One of the greatest gifts God has given to His people is the gift of discernment. How we need wise, compassionate discernment in these last days! In *The Discerner*, James Goll lays out before us a clear and concise teaching on having a heart to discern the works of God and the deeds of the enemy. I've not read a better book for preparing us for the days to come. The ones who discern the ways of God will be the ones to lead us into the coming glory. Every pastor, leader, intercessor, and worshipper must read this book. Every believer will be built up and given tools to be a valuable discerner in the days ahead. Buy one for yourself and one for a friend. They will thank you for it!

—*Brian Simmons*
Stairway Ministries
Lead translator, The Passion Translation Project

Dr. James Goll is one of God's chosen and anointed vessels to identify prophets and to grow the prophetic gifts and abilities within the body of Christ. He has skillfully taught and mentored on various aspects of prophetic revelation over the years, and now he introduces a very important component: *The Discerner*. There is very little written about this subject, and yet it is vital for us to understand. Many readers will find themselves defined as "discerners" when they read this book. As always, Dr. James Goll has penned a remarkable work that will continue to teach and train others for generations to come. Well done!

—*Patricia King*
Founder, Patricia King Ministries
www.xpministries.com

James is such an immense treasure trove of wisdom and revelation on everything to do with spiritual seeing and discerning. No matter what level of discernment you presently have, this amazing book will provide an upgrade to the next level. The chapters on your spiritual senses are priceless. It is all connected to growing in intimacy with God—and that will be the fruit of your reading this wonderful book.

—*Johnny Enlow*
International speaker and author, *The Seven Mountain Renaissance*

The need for discernment within the church is of paramount importance. James Goll does a brilliant job of unpacking this subject with eloquence and deep revelations that have been written with such truth and clarity. This book is a prophetic tool for believers to get equipped in the area of spiritual discernment and hearing the voice of God. I enjoyed every page and found that I couldn't put the book down because I was learning at a deeper level. James is such a deep well, and when it comes to teaching, he is stellar. I truly believe that this is the best book I have read on this subject and highly recommend it. Thank you, James, for being such a powerful prophetic voice in this generation.

—*Alex Seeley*
Speaker and writer
Co-pastor, The Belonging Co, Nashville, TN

James Goll is not just a dear friend; I consider him to be one of profound mind and insight in relation to prophetic perception. As the church continues to move forward into the intention of God for its future, more and more you will be hearing of the need for a Pentecostal and charismatic "Theology of Discernment." As people who believe in the fullness of the Spirit, our comprehension of the process of perception and discernment is influenced by our encounters with God the Father's threefold cord that is never to be separated: the Holy Spirit, the Son of God, and the Scriptures. Within the interrelationship of the three, we as God's company of prophetic and kingly priests are coming to terms with how the entire purpose of discernment has to issue in godly responses and actions that bring about God's desired results. James's newest release, *The Discerner*, gives us all a seat at the table where this conversation is taking place—and will continue to take place and expand as we move forward into the future Jesus has prepared for us. My thanks to James for taking on this topic. As you read, you will discover how James's brilliance shines on every page!

—*Dr. Mark J. Chironna*
Church On The Living Edge
Mark Chironna Ministries, Longwood, FL

James Goll is a longtime dear friend and trusted prophet in my life and in the life of my ministry. James is not only a personal gift to me, but also a gift to the body of Christ, bringing much-needed prophetic vision, scholarship, and wisdom—strengthening and equipping us for the always-timely ministry of the Holy Spirit.

James is a one-of-a-kind prophet, teacher, and prolific writer. With *The Seer*, he delivered a groundbreaking book on the seer gift, releasing many into greater understanding, appreciation, and application of their anointing. Now, with *The Discerner*, James has again led us to another level of insight. When operating in the prophetic, there is the revelation, the interpretation, and the application of what has been revealed. The sharpening of our discernment takes us beyond just revelation to operating effectively in divine wisdom, which helps us not only to perceive and receive from the Lord, but also to practice and activate that prophetic wisdom with clarity.

As believers, we cannot afford to live without the necessary discernment to distinguish between the voice of God, the voice of the enemy, and our own voice. *The Discerner* is a very timely work that will impart truth and bring instruction as to how we might have the mind of Christ (1 Corinthians 2:16) in every situation.

—*Dr. Ché Ahn*
President, Harvest International Ministry
Founding Pastor, HROCK Church, Pasadena, CA
International Chancellor, Wagner University

JAMES W. GOLL

AUTHOR OF NATIONAL BEST SELLER *THE SEER*

THE
DISCERNER

WHITAKER
HOUSE

THE DISCERNER:

Hearing, Confirming, and Acting on Prophetic Revelation

James W. Goll
God Encounters Ministries
P.O. Box 1653
Franklin, TN 37065
www.godencounters.com • www.jamesgoll.com
info@godencounters.com • invitejames@godencounters.com

ISBN: 978-1-62911-902-1 • eBook ISBN: 978-1-62911-903-8
Printed in the United States of America
© 2017 by James W. Goll

Whitaker House
1030 Hunt Valley Circle
New Kensington, PA 15068
www.whitakerhouse.com

Library of Congress Cataloging-in-Publication Data

Names: Goll, Jim W., author.
Title: The discerner : hearing, confirming, and acting on prophetic revelation / James W. Goll.
Description: New Kensington, PA : Whitaker House, 2017. | Includes bibliographical references. |
Identifiers: LCCN 2017039370 (print) | LCCN 2017041281 (ebook) | ISBN 9781629119038 (E-book) | ISBN 9781629119021 (trade pbk. : alk. paper)
Subjects: LCSH: Revelation—Christianity. | Discernment (Christian theology) | Prophecy—Christianity.
Classification: LCC BT127.3 (ebook) | LCC BT127.3 .G64 2017 (print) | DDC 234/.13—dc23
LC record available at https://lccn.loc.gov/2017039370

1 2 3 4 5 6 7 8 9 10 11 **LⱯ** 24 23 22 21 20 19 18 17

DEDICATION

As I pondered and prayed over the dedication for this particular book, two people came to my mind. Both of them have been friends and peers, and yet also spiritual leaders and advisers who have spoken into my life many times over many years. In gratitude and as an act of honor, I wish to dedicate *The Discerner* to influential prophetess Cindy Jacobs, and to Ché Ahn, one of the most significant apostles in this generation. Both of their lives have touched me deeply, and I have needed and valued their discernment. Thank you for investing in my life for so many years!

ACKNOWLEDGMENTS

Over the years, the Lord has graced me to walk with a company of people who have cheered for me, prayed for me, challenged me, and assisted me in many practical and spiritual ways. It has been said that a successful person surrounds himself with people with greater skills than he himself possesses. That is definitely true in my case. I want to acknowledge and honor a few of these stellar people.

First, hats off to Kathy Deering, my writing assistant in more projects than I can count. This excellent writer-editor knows my distinct voice thoroughly; she takes the raw ingredients of my outlines, visionary goals, and transcripts, and brings forth a final product that I am not capable of creating on my own.

Next, I want to thank a friend who believes in me so much that he will listen to me as I rattle on and on. Don Milam has known the path of life that I walk, and he hangs in there with me through thick and thin, championing my plans, purposes, and pursuits.

Third, I wish to thank the staff and board of God Encounters Ministries. I have two board members who have been with me longer than I can remember: Dr. William (Bill) Greenman and Dr. John Mark Rodgers. For them, "thank you" is an inadequate statement. The core of my ministry staff—Jeffrey Thompson, Kay Durham, Don

Clark, and Tyler Goll—have also served me well for these many years, and their excellence and faithfulness mean the world to me. The unity in diversity that we share in our board and staff is what a true dream team looks like!

Thanks also go to Bob Whitaker Jr. for his big heart, for opening the doors of Whitaker House so widely to me. Bob, it is an honor to walk with you and your gracious staff. May the Lord bless each and every one of you!

CONTENTS

FOREWORD

James W. Goll is a leader with a prophetic voice that has shaped this generation. True to his prophetic instincts, he has written a book that is powerful in its timing. From the moment I picked up the manuscript, I could not put it down.

The number one weapon the devil deploys in the last days isn't the mark of the beast, radical Islam, or a nuclear holocaust. His number one weapon is deception. The chief description of Satan's activity in the book of Revelation is that he is "the deceiver of the whole world" whose primary activity is accomplished as he "goes forth to deceive the nations." (See Revelation 12:9; 20:8.) If his number one weapon is deception, the number one gift most needed (and most frequently absent) in the body of Christ is what James Goll writes about here—*discerning of spirits!*

The Lord spoke to James when he was a young pastor and said one sentence that impacted his life: "Your end-time worldview will determine your lifestyle." For James, it does not matter what your particular view of the end is, as long as you are advancing in the activity of the kingdom—reaping the end-time harvest and making disciples of nations. This quality of life can happen only when you are distinguishing the voice of God from the counterfeit. I like how James puts it:

At this point in time, every act of spiritual warfare is leading up to an end-time battle. It behooves every one of us to become discerners who, like the ancient priests of Zadok (see Ezekiel 44:15–23), not only can tell the difference between the holy and the profane, but can teach others as well. We learn to live by Jesus's Sermon on the Mount (see Matthew 5–7), and we teach it to others, too, most often by our actions more than our words. Relation. Revelation. Incarnation. This is our aim; this is our goal! When we receive and discern revelation from God, we become a word from God that penetrates the darkness by turning on the light.

James does a masterful job of detailing how you can surrender all your senses to the Holy Spirit so you can see, hear, feel, taste, smell, and know—with a deep inner knowing—the Spirit of God. He also exposes the spirit of deception and how it operates, outlining the traps and influences it uses to try to set you up for offense or error. He shows you how to *"test the spirits to see whether they are from God"* (1 John 4:1) as he explains, "The unseen supernatural reality around us is populated with both angels and demons, and human beings are notoriously poor at telling the difference between good spirits and bad ones."

James is an experienced guide and teacher who has not only crafted an easy-to-read and informative handbook for your journey, but has also infused his own intercessory spirit into the chapters, closing each segment with a prayer written especially so that you can lock into the revelation.

As you read this book, pray that Jesus will enable you to *receive* His revelation and to *discern* His message out of the chaos of many competing voices surrounding your life. Then He will enable you to *become* the revelation of that which you are hearing! The ability to discern truth and discern error is the path that leads you into the "all" that God has planned for your life. If you are like me, you will mark this book up and refer to it again and again.

—*Lance Wallnau*
Founder, Lance Learning Group
Author, *God's Chaos Candidate:*
Donald J. Trump and the American Unraveling

INTRODUCTION:
THE PLUMB LINE

I often refer to myself as being like the prophet Amos, due to my similar obscure background and the nature of my prophetic calling. I grew up in Cowgill, Missouri, which had a population of 259 at that time, and is now even smaller. My family was not prestigious. No famous person has ever come from Cowgill, and there are no mega-churches or institutions of higher learning there. It is a community in farm country, where people work hard for a living. In other words, absolutely nothing in my geographical, familial, or social background could have prepared me for the prophetic commission that I have been pursuing for my entire adult life. But as prophet Cindy Jacobs likes to say, "God knows!"

Back in Old Testament Judah, Amos started out as a "nobody," too—his family was not part of the nobility, he had never been associated with any school of the prophets, and he didn't grow up in urbane surroundings but in a rural setting where he took care of sheep:

> *I was no prophet, nor was I a son of a prophet, but I was a sheep-breeder and a tender of sycamore fruit. Then the LORD took me*

as I followed the flock, and the Lord *said to me, "Go, prophesy to*
My people Israel." (Amos 7:14–15 nkjv)

Amos had never expected to hear God's voice, and he had not anticipated becoming a prophet. However, he obeyed his prophetic calling, and he applied himself to learning what he needed to know in order to be faithful to that calling. He is best known for making public a word about how God was setting a "plumb line" in the nation of Israel to measure the truth and righteousness of the people and their rulers. The Spirit of God gave him this vision:

The Lord was standing by a wall that had been built true to plumb,
with a plumb line in his hand. And the Lord *asked me, "What*
do you see, Amos?" "A plumb line," I replied. Then the Lord said,
"Look, I am setting a plumb line among my people Israel; I will
spare them no longer." (Amos 7:7–8)

God's plumb line is all-important, not only for aligning crooked human life with His perfect uprightness, but also for discerning His voice in the first place. In the midst of all the noise of the world, we need to be able to distinguish God's voice clearly. God wants you to know what He is saying, even if you never need to wear a prophet's mantle in public.

Like Amos, I work hard to bring a plumb line that can help the people of God do everything according to the word of the Lord. Whether I write books or conduct seminars or lead prayer gatherings, I endeavor to operate to the best of my ability according to what He has taught me. My primary resource, of course, is the Word of God, the Bible. But years of personal experience have made a huge difference in how I have learned to apply the Word. The Holy Spirit is always active, and I try always to remain on the alert for His stirrings. The Spirit is our best Teacher, and even as I present in this book what I have learned about receiving and discerning what God reveals to His people, I want to be sensitive to new insights and new ways of communicating the truth.

Reading the twelve chapters of *The Discerner* will take you on a journey of discovery into God's revelation for us today—a journey I myself have taken. I want to pass on to you what has been passed down to me. (In relating this journey, I have learned new things along the way, too!) The first six chapters explain how you can receive revelation from God through your natural senses, such as sight and hearing, and also how to open yourself up to supernatural senses through which you can know even better what God wants to show you. Chapters seven through twelve bring the art of discernment home. You will learn what to do when Satan tries to infiltrate God's message, and you will be able to identify a model of a healthy, balanced, dynamic, discerning life of faith.

Each of us needs to become a *discerner*—no matter what our personal background or specific gift or function in the body of Christ. Although some believers are especially gifted as prophets, *every* follower of Jesus receives the gifts of revelation and discernment. And every believer needs to use them! In fact, without discernment and sensitivity to the Holy Spirit, we cannot progress in our use of any of the gifts and callings.

In the final analysis, developing discernment is not so much about knowing the future as it is about bringing the kingdom of God to bear on the time and place in which you live. The gospel of John begins with the words, *"The Word became flesh and dwelt among us…, full of grace and truth"* (John 1:14 NKJV), referring to the coming of Jesus Christ to earth. In a very real way, you and I bring God's Word to dwell in the midst of the world as we remain sensitive to the flow of His Spirit. Through our relationship with God, we receive revelation. And as we bring that revelation to the world around us, we actually incarnate His Word in our very ordinary lives—just as Amos did. Please join me in a "plumb line course"—*The Discerner*.

Divine downloads ahead! Get ready!

SECTION ONE:
RECEIVING REVELATION

In this first section, I tackle the whole issue of receiving revelation, although this is not something you can learn only from a book. It is much deeper than that; it has to do with your personal relationship with God.

In *The Normal Christian Life*, Watchman Nee wrote, "I must first have the sense of God's possession of me before I can have the sense of His presence with me."[1] God created human beings with physical senses, powers of perception that enable us to discern the environment in which we live—both natural and spiritual. The senses that we will explore in the first half of this book are seeing, hearing, feeling, tasting, and smelling—as well as a sixth sense, "knowing." All of your senses will be activated and enhanced as they are surrendered to their Creator, who designed you to function at a high level of spiritual sensitivity to the world around you.

Chapter 1 addresses the matter of surrendering to God and allowing Him to possess you, which is the pathway into His presence where you can receive revelation without hindrance. The kind of surrendering I am talking about is not like capitulation to an adversary; it is simply

1. *The Collected Works of Watchman Nee* (Anaheim, CA: Living Streams, 1993), 71.

yielding yourself to God and complying with His will. Revelation flows more quickly and easily through a yielded vessel. Higher realms of glory are available to those who humbly surrender themselves to the Holy Spirit.

Chapter 2 deals with developing your spiritual eyes to see as God sees. There is much happening around us, but we do not often perceive it. We will search the many layers of the seer gift, and I will explain how you can enter more fully into that gift.

Chapter 3 introduces the realm of hearing. As Jesus expressed in John 16:13–15, a significant aspect of the ministry of the Spirit is *listening* to the Father and the Son (*"whatever He hears He will speak"* verse 13 NKJV), and we should follow His example. It takes two people to communicate. I emphasize not only the fact that communication is a two-way street, but also that we should spend more time listening to God than talking to Him.

In chapter 4, we explore the spiritual equivalent to the physical sense of touch, the sense of feeling (our feelings or emotional responses to the environment around us). My goal is to show you that the sense of feeling is a sort of emotional and spiritual braille-reader—it can help you pick up on signals that your other senses might miss. I explain what blocks spiritual sensitivity and how you can become more finely tuned to God's thoughts and desires.

Chapter 5 covers taste and smell. As to the spiritual sense of taste, the Bible makes it clear that it is referring to discernment and distinguishing between good and evil. Scripture is filled with references to the sense of taste. For example, in Psalm 34:8 we read, *"Taste and see that the LORD is good."* Taste and smell are closely associated with one another, and as we exercise our senses, we can also derive significance from what certain scents and odors symbolize, whether holy or unholy.

In chapter 6, I dive into the sixth "sense"—knowing, or spiritual impressions. Since not all thoughts come from God, I give you tips on discerning the difference between a divine impression and a random thought. Additionally, as a believer, it is essential for you to recognize that you have the mind of Christ. (See 1 Corinthians 2:16.) I want to help you understand what to do with knowledge that comes from God, so that you can walk in divine intelligence.

Let's move forward now into the realm of receiving revelation.

1

SURRENDERING YOUR SENSES TO THE HOLY SPIRIT

"Solid food is for the mature, who because of practice have their senses trained to discern good and evil."
—Hebrews 5:14 (NASB)

As a kid growing up in a small town in Missouri, I loved watching programs on our little black-and-white television set. I would watch them for as long as I was allowed, and the picture never seemed dull, lifeless, or lacking in clarity. But when, suddenly, along with the humblest of families, we too upgraded to a color TV, the programs came alive to me in a new way.

Once upon a time, my Christian life looked a lot like our old black-and-white television. The programming and reception were not too bad, and I thought things were going along fine. Then everything shifted unexpectedly, and I have never wanted to go back. Here is what happened.

For some time, I had been getting various brief mental snapshots. I would notice something for a millisecond and think, *Where did that come from? What was that?* It was as if my senses were waking up. Occasionally, I seemed to be able to look deep into a person's being and discern something that would never appear to the naked eye. I remember the first time it occurred. I met a particular church leader, and it was as if I could see diamonds glistening inside his mind, while at the same time I knew what that image meant. I thought about how we all have the mind of Christ (see 1 Corinthians 2:16), and I could tell that this man had God's spirit of wisdom to an exceptional degree. I also felt that this godly wisdom would be used to benefit both the church and secular government.

It was like beginning to see in color instead of in black-and-white. Or, to use the analogy from the verse at the beginning of this chapter, it was like growing out of being a baby who drinks only milk, and sampling solid food instead.

I began to believe that God had more for me, and I started to pay attention to the new "solid foods" He was sending my way—sampling their taste, smell, texture, and appearance, and noticing how they made me feel. I compared my experiences to those of others whom I read about in the Bible or heard about. I wanted to know what was from God and what was from my own imagination or some other source.

PURPOSELY OFFER YOUR SENSES

Each of us has been equipped with five natural senses: sight, hearing, touch, taste, and smell. (There is also something called "common sense," which some of us seem to lack!)

The first step in beginning to discern God's communications with us entails purposely offering our senses to Him. Unless we do this—on an ongoing basis—we will not be able to grow into the maturity of Christ Jesus. If we do not give ourselves to Him intentionally, it will be very difficult to know what He wants us to know and therefore difficult to follow Him obediently.

When we surrender our senses to our Creator, He enhances them. Divine input gets "downloaded" less sluggishly than before. As we practice connecting with Him, He increases our capacity for more. What used to seem impossible becomes achievable. I like to say, "One plus God makes the impossible possible." More than that, it is just plain fun! Hearing from God is a perpetual source of pure joy.

Some people call this "activating your senses," and it is that. But you cannot activate your senses on your own; you must activate them by presenting them to the One who created them. You ask Him to anoint them and activate them for His purposes, in love.

HEARING FROM GOD IS A PERPETUAL SOURCE OF PURE JOY.

Then you practice using them. As the opening verse puts it: *"...who because of practice have their senses trained to discern good and evil."* The prophetic revivalist Jerame Nelson expresses it this way: "It is for you to see, hear, touch, taste and smell in the natural and in the spirit. For the things of the spirit cannot be discerned only in the natural. We need our 'spirit man' to come alive and interact on an entirely different sensory level."[2]

As your senses are activated, you might start receiving "snapshot visions" in your mind's eye, as I did. You might feel God's emotions of anger or compassion. A word or a phrase might come to your mind. Or you might sense or even smell that something is "off." *Huh?* you think. *What could this mean?*

The process of figuring out these communications from God consists of trial and error, just like learning to ride a bicycle. As a father, I remember helping all four of my kids learn to ride a bike, running alongside them with my hand on their back until they could stay up on their own for a few yards. They were so excited when they could finally do it, and when they fell down, I would help them back up.

Likewise, to practice using your senses to discern good and evil will involve some falls. You will not be able to get everything right every time. You might step out boldly, thinking that you are obeying God, only to lose your train of thought, make an incorrect assumption,

---

2. Jerame Nelson, *Activating Your Spiritual Senses* (Chula Vista, CA: Living at His Feet Publications, 2012), 14.

or get embarrassed. Just remember: God loves it every time you step out and practice. And practice pays off! The next few chapters of this book will help you practice using your senses to discern.

Even in their maturity, people who are spiritual giants and who move in a high level of anointing for healing make mistakes. They miss it, and that is OK because it keeps them humble. If they are the "real deal," they will never give up. They will keep practicing, and they will keep cooperating with the Holy Spirit, activating their senses and reaching for the next possibility. I have often pondered what the writer of the book of Hebrews meant when he stated, "*Solid food is for the mature.*" I want to be mature, don't you? For sure, some of maturity comes from this thing called practice.

Discernment involves both discerning good and discerning evil, but many people find that they start out a lot better at one or the other. Some people can pick up on the "diamonds" (as I did), while others see the devils. Maturity entails growth in both: "*...the mature, who because of practice have their senses trained to discern* [both] *good and evil.*"

The word translated "*discern*" in Hebrews 5:14 is *diakrisis* (*Strong's* #1253), which indicates "a distinguishing, deciding, passing sentence on." The same word is used in 1 Corinthians 12:10 in reference to the gift of distinguishing (or discerning) of spirits. *Diakrisis* is related to the word *diakrinō* (*Strong's* #1252), which can indicate "to separate, distinguish, discern one thing from another," or "to doubt, hesitate, waver." The act of discernment, in other words, incorporates some give-and-take, trial and error, presenting a case and disputing it. Only through our practice sessions can we come into greater maturity and eventually overcome even our personal weaknesses. Each of us has them, and they will become exposed to God's beneficial light only if we persist in stepping out in discernment.

With God's help, we have to overcome our fears of practicing discernment. You can't just declare, "Sorry, I just do not want to go there" in regard to where the Spirit is taking you. Do not ever put limits on what God wants to do through you because you are worried about being fooled or beguiled into something "weird" that is not from Him.

You can learn to discern hidden motivating forces, and you can ask God for both wisdom and protection.

During this process, do not follow the crowd, expecting discernment to be a series of thrills. We Christians have been too often persuaded to expect everything to be an exciting breakthrough: "Blind eyes, see—now!" Without a doubt, spiritual breakthroughs are real and valuable. But it takes discernment to know when God wants to achieve an immediate breakthrough—not to mention how He wants to achieve it. Sometimes, insisting on having a breakthrough in any area of our lives just reveals the presence of our human impatience. (It can even lead to greed, as in the case of becoming involved in a shady financial scheme in order to fast-track monetary gain.) We can be way too gullible, and we often want everything to be so easy.

PRESENT *YOURSELF* TO GOD

Every one of us has a spirit, a soul, and a body. As tripartite human beings, we cannot separate these elements from each other. Having been made in the image and likeness of the triune God, our three aspects of being are so well-integrated that we cannot divide them. We sometimes talk about them as if they do not overlap and blend, but such compartmentalization is useful only when it helps us to comprehend the distinct capabilities we possess as humans.

Additionally, because our senses cannot be separated from our spirit, soul, and body, we must surrender not only our senses to God, but really our entire being. Paul wrote to the Roman church about this:

> *Therefore I urge you, brethren, by the mercies of God, to present your bodies a living and holy sacrifice, acceptable to God, which is your spiritual service of worship. And do not be conformed to this world, but be transformed by the renewing of your mind, so that you may prove what the will of God is, that which is good and acceptable and perfect.* (Romans 12:1–2 NASB)

Paul also cautioned the believers about presenting themselves to anything *but* God:

> *Do not go on presenting the members of your body to sin as instruments of unrighteousness; but present yourselves to God as those alive from the dead, and your members as instruments of righteousness to God.... I am speaking in human terms because of the weakness of your flesh. For just as you presented your members as slaves to impurity and to lawlessness, resulting in further lawlessness, so now present your members as slaves to righteousness, resulting in sanctification.* (Romans 6:13, 19 NASB)

In presenting your physical body to the Lord, you also surrender your senses, your cognitive faculties (your mind), and your spiritual intuitions. It all comes from Him in the first place, so why should we ever lay claim to any of it as our personal property; why should we reserve anything as off-limits to Him? And why do we continue to present the members of our body to sin?

Whatever we have not presented to God remains subject to something besides God. "Enslaved" is not too strong a term to use. If you have allowed your senses to become addicted to anything—impure sexual stimulation, music, alcohol, drugs or other substances, or even religious activities—they are unavailable to the Spirit of God. Consequently, your discernment is hampered or shut down.

> ## WHATEVER WE HAVE NOT PRESENTED TO GOD REMAINS SUBJECT TO SOMETHING BESIDES GOD.

As long as you are still alive, it is never too late to change. You can surrender the enslaved members of your body to God. The way Paul put it was to say, *"Do not go on presenting the members of your body to sin as instruments of unrighteousness,"* and *"Just as you presented your members as slaves to impurity...so now present your members as slaves to righteousness."* It may be necessary for you to seek help to overcome your addiction, but your situation is never hopeless; you can experience God's fullest life flooding your senses.

You can declare freedom to your own body, soul, and spirit. You can speak to your sight, hearing, touch, taste, and smell, saying, "Senses, become unlocked in the name of Jesus. I declare that you are no longer captive to the patterns of the past; instead, I present you to the one true and holy God for reclamation and purification."

Your physical sense of hearing will become enhanced with a spiritual sense of hearing, and you will begin to hear things from a divine dimension that you have never heard before. Your ordinary sense of sight will become enriched with a spiritual sight by which, as God directs, you will be enabled to see beyond the limits of human vision. Depending on your unique mix of God-given capabilities, your other senses will wake up and take notice of messages they could not perceive before. A whole new world will open up.

To present your whole self to be a slave to purity means stepping free of the hindrances of the past. Instead of unbelief and a dull heart, you step into the living color of vibrant faith. Your heightened senses get activated. It is like putting the keys into the ignition of your discernment. And *"you shall know the truth, and the truth shall make you free"* (John 8:32 NKJV).

It is never a one-time deal. You willingly surrender yourself more and more. You may think you have surrendered your whole being to God's Spirit, but there is layer upon layer upon layer of freedom and activation. We serve an infinite God, you know! This is what it means to be a temple of His Holy Spirit. (See 1 Corinthians 3:16; 6:19.)

GOD MANIFESTS HIMSELF THROUGH US

The Godhead expresses Himself in such a variety of ways that human beings cannot catalog them all. And He manifests Himself through every one of the individual people He has made for His glory; no one is left out:

Now there are varieties of gifts, but the same Spirit. And there are varieties of ministries, and the same Lord. There are varieties of effects, but the same God who works all things in all persons. But to each one is given the manifestation of the Spirit for the common good. (1 Corinthians 12:4–7 NASB)

Notice what it says: "God…works all things in all persons." It does not say, "…in the elite." Most of us compare ourselves with others and feel that we come up short in the gift department. We listen to Bible teachers with national or international platforms and wonder how our little faith walk can ever measure up to theirs. In reality, their job assignment—which is to equip others (like you!) to operate in their spiritual gifts—does not indicate some sort of specially favored status in the church. The body of Christ is composed of all sorts of members, some noticeable and some less noticeable. Far from being a privileged and superior individual, a conference speaker may be more like an index finger in the body of Christ, pointing out truths and giving significance to the giftedness of his or her listeners. Each and every person has a part to play as the Holy Spirit brings the kingdom to bear on the world:

For to one is given the word of wisdom through the Spirit, and to another the word of knowledge according to the same Spirit; to another faith by the same Spirit, and to another gifts of healing by the one Spirit, and to another the effecting of miracles, and to another prophecy, and to another the distinguishing of spirits, to another various kinds of tongues, and to another the interpretation of tongues. But one and the same Spirit works all these things, distributing to each one individually just as He wills. (1 Corinthians 12:8–11 NASB)

Nine spiritual gifts are listed in this passage. You can review each of them in detail in other works, including my book *Releasing Spiritual Gifts Today*[3] and its related study materials. In *The Discerner*, we will be surveying most completely the gift referred to above as "*the distinguishing of spirits*," or discernment, and I will be making a case for the

---

3. James W. Goll, *Releasing Spiritual Gifts Today* (New Kensington, PA: Whitaker House, 2016).

idea that the responsible exercise of any of the spiritual gifts requires an ever-increasing degree of discernment and sensitivity to the Holy Spirit.

GOD GIVES US DEFINING MOMENTS

As each of us follows the Lord, we will encounter defining moments, after which nothing is the same as it was before. Such strategic moments often point us in God's big-picture direction for our future, help to sharpen our discernment, and release spiritual bravery for life's journey. The defining moments will be different for each person. They may occur early or late in life. Some will come in times of crisis, others in times of tranquility.

Early in my marriage, I had a personal encounter with Jesus that changed my life. I refer to it as my "golden anointing." Here is what happened.

I decided to take five days to seek the Lord in a little empty chapel on the campus of Central Missouri State University in Warrensburg, Missouri. The pews of the chapel were equipped with pull-down, kneeling benches, and I slipped down onto one of them.

As I prayed, I did not hear anything, but I *felt* Someone come into the chapel. I felt wind, even though no window or door was open. It was the Spirit of Jesus. He spoke quietly to my spirit for a time, giving me insights and details about a time of transition that was ahead and telling me to turn over my pastoral ministry role to another person. He even told me who that other person was. I assented. It seemed that I needed to be willing to release my current responsibilities so that I could move into new ones.

Then I heard an audible voice: "Arise." Then this command: "Stand up."

This was nuts. There was nobody in the chapel except me. I stood up like a little frozen tin soldier. The fear of the Lord was nearly paralyzing me.

Then He said, "Step out into the aisle."

I raised the question, "Well, why?" but I obeyed. I stepped out into the center aisle of the chapel, between the two ranks of pews.

"Step forward."

I took a little, six-inch step forward. Instantly, the whole room was illuminated with what some people call the glory of God. I know it was not the sunshine from outside. Again, the voice said, "Step forward," and I took another tiny step. Wonder of wonders, I could see Jesus Himself standing in front of me. Now I would call what I was experiencing an open vision. With His beckoning call came an invitation to higher consecration as I took more baby steps forward until I was face-to-face and eye-to-eye with Him.

Then He spoke the same words again: "Step forward." In humility and in the fear of the Lord, with faith and obedience, I took one more step forward. This time, the open manifestation of the vision disappeared because as I took that step, I stepped into Him—and He stepped into me.

The next thing I knew, I was on my knees in consecration and worship. As I looked up, I saw pictures of two people who later became very important in my personal equipping and training: healing evangelist and apostle Mahesh Chavda and seer prophet Bob Jones.

At that moment, I felt a single drop of golden anointing oil land on my head—one drop. Then one more. I looked up again and saw a pitcher over my head, but nothing was coming out of it. The Holy Spirit spoke to me and said, "Today I am giving you two drops of My golden anointing. One is for you, and one you are to give to your wife." He promised me that if I would be faithful with the one drop, a day would come for more of the golden anointing.

I really did not know what He was talking about, but I accepted both the two-drop anointing and the words.

In due time, I went home. I did not tell my wife what had happened until the next day. After I told her about the experience, I took a bottle of cooking oil and anointed her with one drop of it.

To this day, I have never had a repeat of that experience. As far as I know, I am still operating on that one drop of the golden anointing. Therefore, I am sure of one thing: the promise is still good. If I am faithful with the little He has given me (and it has turned out to be such a beneficial anointing), He will someday pour an abundant golden anointing all over my head. Faithfulness always brings increase. That is the promise of Jesus!

I tell you that story because I want to show you that all things are possible for those who belong to God. I have seen Jesus on other occasions, but that first time and every time since, it was all I could take. Reaching from one realm to the next always involves more surrender to the Holy Spirit. But there are always higher realms of glory, higher realms of faith, and higher realms of gifts to reach. Be open to the "more" that God has for you and step into the living color of spiritual discernment.

> REACHING FROM ONE REALM TO THE NEXT ALWAYS INVOLVES MORE SURRENDER TO THE HOLY SPIRIT.

REACHING FOR A HIGHER REALM

What stands out to you from this chapter? Quite likely, God wants to speak to you personally about it.

What action step or steps can you take as a result of something you have read here? Remember that information without application (action) leads to frustration, but inspiration plus application leads to transformation.

Your first action step may be as basic as praying a prayer of surrender. God does not need to be a lip-reader, because He is a heart-reader. But He loves to hear your voice speaking to Him. I encourage you to reach into the deepest place in your heart and to say to Him, "Yes,

Lord, I surrender my whole self to You, including my senses. I long to know You better."

You are growing even now as you surrender your senses—it is not "if" or "maybe." Even if you are somewhat overwhelmed by the Holy Spirit, to the point that you cannot express yourself, or even if you are afraid of what might happen when your discernment increases, trust Him to guide and protect you. Even if you have had a close encounter with the enemy that you would rather not repeat, please do not shut the door to the Holy Spirit. Do not dictate to the Lord, "That's not for me, thanks. I don't want to get too good at discerning if it means another run-in with Satan." Be bold and confident in the Lord. He will not leave you on your own.

It is all right if your prayer of surrender is not very eloquent; God can read your heart's desire. I think of the old hymn "I Surrender All." The words go like this:

> All to Jesus I surrender,
> All to Him I freely give;
> I will ever love and trust Him,
> In His presence daily live.
>> I surrender all,
>> I surrender all;
>> All to Thee, my blessed Savior,
>> I surrender all.
> All to Jesus I surrender,
> Lord, I give myself to Thee;
> Fill me with Thy love and power,
> Let Thy blessing fall on me.[4]

I invite you to join me in new surrender to the Holy Spirit as we expect our senses to become activated and sharpened for Jesus's sake.

---

4. Judson W. Van DeVenter, "All to Jesus I Surrender" ("I Surrender All"), 1896.

PRAYER OF A DISCERNING HEART

Here I am, Lord. All that I am and all that I hope to be, I surrender to You. I present to You my body, soul, and spirit, with all of their natural and supernatural senses. May they be useful to You as instruments for accomplishing Your will on earth. For Jesus Christ's sake and in His name, amen.

2

SEEING:
"THE EYES OF YOUR HEART"

"I pray that the eyes of your heart may be enlightened, so that you will know what is the hope of His calling, what are the riches of the glory of His inheritance in the saints, and what is the surpassing greatness of His power toward us who believe."
—Ephesians 1:18–19 (NASB)

When the apostle Paul prayed the above prayer for the believers in the city of Ephesus, he had just declared, *"Having heard of the faith in the Lord Jesus which exists among you and your love for all the saints..."* (Ephesians 1:15 NASB). Even with their noteworthy faith and love, Paul knew that they had only scratched the surface of mining God's inexhaustible riches. He wanted *"the eyes of [their] hearts,"* or their spiritual sense of sight, to be opened still more to heavenly things.

Forty years ago, I began to pray Ephesians 1:17–19 every day, and I continued for ten straight years, figuring that if such a commendable apostolic church as that of the Ephesians—whose members followed Christ in a city filled with idolatry—needed this prayer, I needed it much more. Today, even having the entire Bible at our fingertips, along with many opportunities for strong fellowship and good teaching, we are just as limited in our human weaknesses as the Ephesians were— and the world around us is just as daunting and trauma-filled as ever. I continue to pray this passage from Ephesians often. Why? In our day, I believe I need the impact of this prayer even more than I did four decades ago. We all need to regularly pray this prayer for ourselves, for our families and friends, for our leaders, and for our influencers.

SEEING WITH THE EYES OF OUR HEART

Paul's phrase *"the eyes of your heart"* has become familiar to many of us, so we often just skip past it when reading this passage, without considering what it means. But let's stop and think about it for a moment. How does your heart have eyes?

Other Bible translations shed light on the meaning of this expression. For example, it is rendered *"the eyes of your understanding"* in the King James and *New King James* versions. Obviously, *"heart"* does not refer to the muscle in your chest that pumps blood to circulate throughout your body. It means your inner self, your spirit.

And when Paul refers to the *"eyes"* of your heart, he means your spirit-eyes. With the eyes of your spirit, you can catch sight of and comprehend the deepest things of the kingdom—namely, the hope of Jesus's calling to each of us as part of His church, the glorious riches that belong to us as coheirs with Christ, and the continuing displays of God's mighty power in our lives. All this is too much to comprehend, and yet Paul prays that the Ephesians—and we, by extension—may be able to grasp it.

In chapter 1 of this book, we touched on the idea that we are not meant to remain as earthbound as we might think, because even as I live my daily life here in Franklin, Tennessee, and you live yours in Baltimore, Maryland; London, England; Cape Town, South Africa; or anywhere else, we are seated with Christ at the right hand of the Father in heaven. (See Ephesians 1:20; 2:6.) As we worship Him, we ascend to Him in the heavenlies. Yet we are still physically here on earth. Each of us is composed of body, soul, and spirit, and God wants to enhance and integrate all of our senses on every level so that He can dwell more fully in us and we in Him.

Again, as we are learning how to rule and reign with Christ in the heavenly places, we are presenting to Him everything we can present—and that includes every level of our seeing ability, along with all our other senses. We say, "Here I am, Lord. Take me! Enlighten the eyes of my heart. Open my eyes to the magnificence of Your kingdom."

> WITH THE EYES OF YOUR SPIRIT,
> YOU CAN CATCH SIGHT OF
> AND COMPREHEND THE DEEPEST THINGS
> OF THE KINGDOM.

HOW DO YOU SEE?

What is the status of your spiritual sight? Just as our natural eyes can suffer various hindrances to perfect vision, so can the eyes of our spirit. In the realm of physical sight, people can be nearsighted, farsighted, or partially or completely blind. They can experience certain distortions in their vision. They can see unwanted spots or "floaters," or have an annoying film over their eyes, impairing their sight. They can have problems seeing colors or distinguishing between hues, or they can have poor night vision. We do not have all of these problems at the same time; however, many of us are accustomed to having vision that is weaker in some regards than in others.

Does the Holy Spirit want to leave the eyes of our hearts with similar impaired vision? Apparently not. God wants us to see spiritual realities clearly.

The more you offer prayers such as the one above from Ephesians, and affiliate yourself with other believers who do, the more clearly you will be able to see into heavenly realms. Where learning about spiritual seeing is concerned, I want you to appreciate the fact that there is an abundance of resources available to assist us: books from other authors who have developed their spiritual sight;[5] books like this one and many others that I have written, such as *The Seer* and *Dream Language*; sermons; and seminars—all forms of biblical instruction—as well as our rubbing shoulders with others who have given themselves to a similar pursuit. You could call it a "spiritual culture," this association with a company of people who belong to Jesus and who desire to strengthen the clarity of the eyes of their hearts.

SPIRITUAL DISCOVERY

In the early 1970s, when I was first starting to learn about and grow in hearing God, books and other teaching materials on the subject were scarce. I went first to the Word of God, in particular to the apostolic epistles of the New Testament. Since the book of Ephesians stood out to me, I concentrated a lot of my attention on it, and that is when I first noticed Paul's prayer in chapter 1.

Building on what I learned from the Bible and from friends, I began to exercise my "seer sense," consulting the Holy Spirit every step of the way. Now I almost take for granted the fact that God shows me things, but then it was all new. And the eyes of my spirit have never (yet, anyway) become as sensitive to the movements of the Holy Spirit as those of the late John Wimber. In corporate settings, he would announce things like this: "I see the Holy Spirit coming right now like the sea flowing across the land. A light is starting over there, and it is moving across people in this direction." And sure enough, the people would begin to respond to the powerful glory of God in a wave—something they could not have done as smoothly on their own, even if they had rehearsed it ahead of time.

I found out that although there are no shortcuts in discipleship and growing in maturity, it is possible for what was the hard-to-reach "ceiling" for the previous generation to become the "floor," or baseline, for the current generation. I could see that Paul understood this reality; he wanted all of Jesus's people—from Ephesus to the ends of the earth—to embark on a continuously expanding voyage of spiritual

---

5. See the "Recommended Reading" section at the back of this book.

discovery. Thus, I found mentors such as Mike Bickle and Bob Jones in places like Kansas City, which was not too far from where my wife and I lived. I watched how they operated in their seer giftings, and I noticed the many different ways in which the eyes of their spirits could see.

But they also introduced me to ideas such as dream language,[6] declaring truth boldly, and much more. I ended up spending hours and hours with Bob, praying for people. That gave me a lot of first-hand experience in observing a seer at work. So many things are better "caught" than taught. I received much instruction in the ways of the Spirit by association, observation, and impartation. Thanks to mentors like Bob, and of course to the ongoing work of the Holy Spirit, the seeing capacity of the eyes of my heart has never stopped expanding. I recommend that you, too, frequently offer that prayer from Ephesians—because it is still working in my life! "More, Lord!"

> IT IS POSSIBLE FOR WHAT WAS THE HARD-TO-REACH "CEILING" FOR THE PREVIOUS GENERATION TO BECOME THE "FLOOR," OR BASELINE, FOR THE CURRENT GENERATION.

PROPHETS AND SEERS IN THE BIBLE

In both the Old and New Testaments, we can find examples of spiritual gifts and offices in operation, including those designated *prophet* and *seer*. Most people see no real distinction between the roles of those who carried these titles. Indeed, the modes of operation in these gifts overlap greatly. However, from what I have observed firsthand about those who exercise prophetic gifts, I think the following distinction is applicable: while all true seers are prophets, not all prophets are seers. I expand on this idea more fully below. As we continue with this

6. The realm of dreams and visions as an avenue for receiving divine revelation.

discussion, please keep in mind that you do not have to be acknowl-edged as a prophet or a seer in order to hear God. All you have to be is a follower of the Lord Jesus Christ.

In the Old Testament, the Hebrew word most often translated "prophet" is *nabiy'*, which generally refers to an inspired hearer and speaker. We may distinguish *nabiy'* from the two Hebrew words trans-lated "seer," *ra'ah* and *chozeh*, which indicate someone whose inspira-tion is primarily visual. Seers receive information from God but do not necessarily communicate it as prophets do. The different terms also reflect the dimensions of the prophetic gift being emphasized. As I wrote in *The Seer*,

> Within the overall realm of the prophet lies the particular and distinctive realm of *the seer*.... The word *seer* describes a particular type of prophet who receives a particular type of prophetic revelation or impartation....
>
> ...The prophet is the *communicative* dimension, and the seer is the *receptive* dimension. Whereas *nabiy'* emphasizes the active work of the prophet in speaking forth a message from God, *ra'ah* and *chozeh* focus on the experience or means by which the prophet "sees or perceives" that message. The first places emphasis on a prophet's relationship with the people; the second places emphasis on a prophet's revelatory relationship with God.[7]

Let us now look at some Old Testament Scriptures in which *nabiy'*, *ra'ah*, and *chozeh* appear. First, consider these four "prophet" Scriptures:

> *I will raise up for them a prophet like you from among their fellow Israelites, and I will put my words in his mouth. He will tell them everything I command him.*   (Deuteronomy 18:18)

---

7. James Goll, *The Seer*, expanded edition (Shippensburg, PA: Destiny Image, 2012), 28–29. Emphasis is in the original.

The LORD said to Moses: "See, I have made you as God to Pharaoh, and Aaron your brother shall be your prophet."
(Exodus 7:1 NKJV)

You [Moses] shall speak to him [Aaron] and put words in his mouth; I will help both of you speak and will teach you what to do. He will speak to the people for you, and it will be as if he were your mouth and as if you were God to him. (Exodus 4:15–16)

"Before I formed you in the womb I knew you; before you were born I sanctified you; I ordained you a prophet to the nations."... Then the LORD put forth His hand and touched my mouth, and the LORD said to me: "Behold, I have put My words in your mouth." (Jeremiah 1:5, 9 NKJV)

Next, take a look at these four "seer" Scriptures:

Formerly in Israel, if someone went to inquire of God, they would say, "Come, let us go to the seer [ra'ah]," because the prophet of today used to be called a seer [ra'ah]. (1 Samuel 9:9)

King Hezekiah and his officials ordered the Levites to praise the LORD with the words of David and of Asaph the seer [chozeh]. So they sang praises with gladness and bowed down and worshipped. (2 Chronicles 29:30)

Before David got up the next morning, the word of the LORD had come to Gad the prophet, David's seer [chozeh].
(2 Samuel 24:11)

At that time Hanani the seer [ra'ah] came to Asa king of Judah, and said to him: "Because you have relied on the king of Syria, and have not relied on the LORD your God, therefore the army of the king of Syria has escaped from your hand.... For the eyes of the LORD run to and fro throughout the whole earth, to show Himself strong on behalf of those whose heart is loyal to Him. In this you

have done foolishly; therefore from now on you shall have wars."
Then Asa was angry with the seer [ra'ah], and put him in prison,
for he was enraged at him because of this.

(2 Chronicles 16:7, 9–10 NKJV)

The passage from Exodus 7 interests me in particular because
Moses, who had a stammering problem and who was hesitant to speak
publicly (see Exodus 4:10), was a seer, while his brother Aaron served as
his prophetic mouthpiece. This illustrates the fact that much of what a
seer does is behind-the-scenes in relational contexts rather than in public
ministry. Seers often help give insight to someone who has a platform.

Another fascinating passage can be found in the book of
Habakkuk:

I will stand on my guard post and station myself on the rampart;
and I will keep watch to see what He will speak to me, and how I
may reply when I am reproved. Then the LORD answered me and
said, "Record the vision and inscribe it on tablets, that the one who
reads it may run. For the vision is yet for the appointed time; it
hastens toward the goal and it will not fail. Though it tarries, wait
for it; for it will certainly come, it will not delay."

(Habakkuk 2:1–3 NASB)

How will Habakkuk "watch to see what the Lord will speak"? It
does not mean he will lip-read what the Lord says. But how else can
you "watch" speech? Speech is meant to be heard, isn't it? Unless the
speaker is using sign language, that is. And that is actually the key: you
watch for God's *signs* to know what He is saying, because God speaks
through signs and wonders, as well as through words.

And you watch in silence, attentively. Quietness is the incubation
bed of revelation. (See, for example, Isaiah 30:15.) You quiet yourself
inwardly as you wait upon the Lord. This focuses the eyes of your heart
on God, raises your level of expectancy, and makes you more fully open
to receive something from Him. Even if you are an extrovert, you need
to heed the Spirit's call to *"come aside"* (Mark 6:31 NKJV) and to nurture
quiet receptivity. Turn off your computer and your television. Put away
your phone. Dedicate your "seeing" time to Him, without distractions.

Also, get ready to record what you see, as Habakkuk modeled for us. He had to inscribe his prophetic words on clay tablets, whereas you will use pen and paper or digital devices. If you do not get into the habit of recording your little glimpses of what God is saying, you will forget them, and valuable words from God may be lost forever. In Habakkuk's words: *"Record the vision and inscribe it on tablets, that the one who reads it may run. For the vision is yet for the appointed time"* (Habakkuk 2:2–3 NASB). Each one of us is going to perceive more in the Spirit than we can possibly see fulfilled in our lifetimes, and somebody else may have to pick up the baton.

Writing (or making an audio recording) of your own visions and impressions also enables you to evaluate the validity of what you have seen, as you hold it up against Scripture and your knowledge of God's character. Not everything that captures your attention comes from Him!

This is not to say that everything you record needs to be shared with others. Ask the Lord to show you if, when, and how you should share your visions. Just because you see something does not obligate you to talk about it.

> QUIETNESS IS THE INCUBATION BED
> OF REVELATION.

IMPARTATION OF THE SEER GIFT

The prophet Elisha was a seer, and he enabled others to be seers as well. We might do the same for other people. You may remember this story:

> *When the servant of the man of God got up and went out early the next morning, an army with horses and chariots had surrounded the city. "Oh no, my lord! What shall we do?" the servant asked. "Don't be afraid," the prophet answered. "Those who are with us are more than those who are with them." And Elisha prayed,*

"Open his eyes, LORD, so that he may see." Then the LORD opened the servant's eyes, and he looked and saw the hills full of horses and chariots of fire all around Elisha.　　　　(2 Kings 6:15–17)

With the eyes of his heart, Elisha could see the massed forces of heaven, but they were completely invisible to the eyes of his frightened servant. So Elisha prayed that God would open his servant's eyes to the spiritual reality, and He did.

In her book *Developing Your Five Spiritual Senses*, my friend Patricia King states the following concerning this interchange between Elisha and the servant: "Elisha's servant could not see into this realm. He was fearful and despairing. Elisha prayed to God that his servant's eyes would open to see into the invisible realm. As a result, this servant was given spiritual vision enabling him to see the armies of God that were there to defend them."[8]

Thus, someone who sees can pray for someone who does not, and when that person's eyes are opened, the wonder of the sign from God will be multiplied. This is an act of impartation, plain and simple. Such a prayer is not complicated. It reflects a close relationship with the Holy Spirit and a straightforward dependency upon Him.

Every time we help someone see into God's unknown realm, we enhance the culture of faith. Faith replaces fear when we see the armies of heaven—and more. Greater is He who is in us (the Spirit) than the one (Satan) who is in the world (see 1 John 4:4); and God is always willing to expand our natural senses by the anointing of His Spirit so that we can move in maximum faith.

SPIRITUAL SIGHT AND DISCERNMENT

DISCERNING HUMAN SPIRITS

Jesus, who exemplifies every spiritual ability, was a seer. He saw His future disciple Nathaniel spiritually before He saw him with His physical eyes:

8. Patricia King, *Developing Your Five Spiritual Senses* (Maricopa, AZ: XP Publishing, 2014), 47.

When Jesus saw Nathanael approaching, he said of him, "Here truly is an Israelite in whom there is no deceit." "How do you know me?" Nathanael asked. Jesus answered, "I saw you while you were still under the fig tree before Philip called you." Then Nathanael declared, "Rabbi, you are the Son of God; you are the king of Israel." Jesus said, "You believe because I told you I saw you under the fig tree. You will see greater things than that."

(John 1:47–50)

Jesus not only could see the man Nathanael sitting under the fig tree, but He also could see into Nathanael's heart. Jesus could evaluate Nathanael's spiritual condition and then declare that this man had no deceptiveness in him.

You and I can grow into this kind of seeing, if we surrender ourselves to God and follow the instruction He gives us along the way. You do not have to be a highly gifted person to do it, just a willing one, yielded to Him.

DISCERNING GOOD AND EVIL FORCES

Many years ago, when our first son was a baby, I began to see more clearly in the Spirit and to discern good and evil. I was definitely hungry for more of God, and I believe that is a key to receiving from Him.[9] For five nights in a row, the Holy Spirit woke me up at two in the morning. I would get out of bed and go into our living room and sit down. Then I would "see" a present, like a Christmas gift, come floating down out of heaven to my lap. Every night, the present was wrapped in a different color of paper and a different color of ribbon: gold paper with a blue ribbon, green paper with a red ribbon, silver paper with a gold ribbon, and so on. All these colors were symbolic, and I understood much of what they represented, but I did not open them. Then, on the fifth night (remembering that the number five represents "grace" in biblical

---

9. If you are a parent, you will know that you pay attention when one of your children pulls on your heart by reaching up to you. You are less likely to interact with the child who is distracted and caught up in other affairs. A good father is inclined to give good gifts to the one who asks.

numerology), I went ahead and opened the present that had been given to me.

Operating in the seer realm, I took hold of the ribbon, untied it, and took the lid off the box. (We all need to do this—to take the lid off God's gifts by faith.) I reached down inside the box and took hold of two objects, thinking, *Whoa…. What's this?* They were glass eyes—two of them. I took one in each hand and placed them on top of my natural eyes, whereupon they seemed to melt right into them.

At that point in time, I had already been seeing in the Spirit to some extent; otherwise, I would have been freaked out by this five-night experience. But after that night, I began to see much better than ever before. I started seeing both good and evil forces. I also started seeing future outpourings of the Spirit, upcoming calamities, and impending natural disasters, including earthquakes. I could understand God's callings and destinies for people and cities. This was God's way of imparting more seer ability to me, and I tried to do a good job of keeping track of what I saw so that I could share my perceptions with others as it was appropriate to do so.

When I say I started to see both good and evil forces, I mean I started *discerning* good and evil more than before. I could identify angels—as well as their evil counterparts, demons. I could distinguish the hand of God in a situation, and I could see Satan's fingerprints, too. I could discern the presence of the Holy Spirit more than before, and I had a higher degree of wisdom regarding what He wanted me to do with what I was seeing.

One purpose of the spiritual gift of discerning of spirits (see 1 Corinthians 12:10) is to detect, expose, and put a halt to the activities of the evil one, for the sake of the welfare of the people of God. An example of this is when Paul unmasked the mixed motives of Simon the magician. (See Acts 13:6–10.) This gift was also in operation when the apostle discerned the evil spirit in the slave girl in Philippi. (See Acts 16:16–18.) She was proclaiming truth, which tended to muddy the process of discernment. Only the Holy Spirit could have revealed that she was being spurred on by a demon for the purpose of foiling the establishment of the good news of the kingdom in that region.

As I learned more about the gift of discerning of spirits, I found that I could more accurately perceive the motivating spirit behind certain words or actions of people, whether holy, demonic, or merely human. Sometimes I somehow "just knew" the significance of what I was seeing. Other times, I had to wait, watching and studying a situation or a person in order to detect the good or bad results of their words or deeds. Since not all spiritual activity comes from God, it is vital for members of the body of Christ to be able to penetrate beyond what seems obvious to the natural eye and human perception.

In all this, my sense of sight was being trained. This level of spiritual seeing and perceiving is like the solid food for mature believers we talked about in the previous chapter: *"Solid food is for the mature, who because of practice have their senses trained to discern good and evil"* (Hebrews 5:14 NASB).

> SINCE NOT ALL SPIRITUAL ACTIVITY
> COMES FROM GOD,
> BELIEVERS MUST BE ABLE TO
> PENETRATE BEYOND
> WHAT SEEMS OBVIOUS TO THE
> NATURAL EYE AND HUMAN PERCEPTION.

REACHING FOR A HIGHER REALM

"Open the Eyes of My Heart" is a contemporary Christian song by Paul Baloche that has been translated into many languages. It is based on the Scripture passage with which we started this chapter, Ephesians 1:18–19, and it is a good prayer to say or sing. God will always answer it.

You can expect God to tailor His answer to your particular situation. That is because your heart is as unique as the way the eyes of your heart will function. The best way to cooperate with the training process of God's Spirit is to keep reaching up to Him and keep seeking more of Him. Like Habakkuk, make a record of what you see, even if it is just a fleeting vision. Pay attention to what you see in your dreams, because they may include "visions of the night" from God. (See Job 33:15.) Learn how to quiet yourself in His presence so you can wait expectantly for what He might show you. Give yourself to Him, body, soul, and spirit, and tell Him that you want the eyes of your spirit to be enlightened.

Look for mentors, and do not be shy about asking a gifted person to pray for you for an impartation of the seer gift. Find good resources that can teach you more about discerning good and evil. Look for testimonies that demonstrate personal experiences of seeing with the eyes of the spirit, and be alert to whatever may spark your attention. When other people tell us about their experiences of seeing with the eyes of their hearts, these stories kindle expectancy in our own hearts. We become open to new experiences of seeing in the Spirit.

Do not forget to worship God as much as possible. Positioning yourself before Him in humble worship proves to be one of the best enhancements to growth in the visionary or seer realm. Just think about John the Beloved when he was in exile on the Isle of Patmos. He was in worship on the Lord's Day when he began to receive the stupendous visions that became the final book of the Bible. (See Revelation 1:9–11.) Worship gets us plugged into heaven better than anything I know, because worship is the whole business of heaven.

PRAYER OF A DISCERNING HEART

Father God, I worship You with my whole being. Once again I surrender myself to You, because You are my Creator; I love You and I trust You. I extend my hands upward, asking for more of Your Holy Spirit. In particular, I surrender my physical and spiritual eyes to You, and I ask for an increase of Your gifting and anointing.

I ask You directly for the ability to see with new eyes. I want to have visions, and I ask You to help me understand them. As I read Your Word, feed me the food of the mature. Increase the spirit of wisdom and revelation in me so that I can see what You see. I want to be more effective for Your purposes.

By the grace of God, I believe that I will receive an increase of visions, dreams, and glimpses of Your glory. I receive whatever You want to give me, in the name of Your Son Jesus. Amen.

3

HEARING: "WHATEVER HE HEARS, HE WILL SPEAK"

"But when He, the Spirit of truth, comes, He will guide you into
all the truth; for He will not speak on His own initiative,
but whatever He hears, He will speak;
and He will disclose to you what is to come."
—John 16:13 (NASB)

What is the ministry of the Holy Spirit?"

When I ask people that question, I get a variety of answers, and they are all correct: "He gives spiritual gifts." "He brings conviction." "He cultivates character and the fruit of the Spirit in people's lives." "He speaks truth and releases comfort—and does so much more."

The Holy Spirit does a lot. However, I have yet to get one particular response: "The ministry of the Holy Spirit is *listening*." Yet that is what Jesus's words in the above Scripture tell us. We do not tend to think of the Holy Spirit as a listener. We may think of our own need to listen to the voice of the Spirit. But apparently we would have nothing to listen for if the Holy Spirit did not first listen to the Father's voice.

That is what the verse says: *"Whatever He hears, He will speak."* He listens before He says anything. In the same way, we need to listen to Him before we open our mouths to declare the word of the Lord.

When Jesus spoke the above words, recorded later by John the Beloved, the Holy Spirit had not yet been given to the disciples because Jesus had not yet ascended to heaven after His resurrection. Now, though, the Spirit of truth has come, and He keeps on coming into the lives of men and women of God everywhere. He comes to do many things, but He always *listens* first. Everything He says or does guides us into a fuller revelation of the Father's heart. He discloses God's plans for the future, pulling aside the curtain to reveal how God intends to bring His kingdom into the world. Only as we learn to listen to the Holy Spirit are we able to join in.

> EVERYTHING THE SPIRIT SAYS
> OR DOES GUIDES US INTO
> A FULLER REVELATION OF
> THE FATHER'S HEART.

LISTEN TO HEAR

Although it sounds almost too obvious to say it, the truth is that you cannot hear the voice of God unless you listen for it. Hearing is one of our five natural senses that God wants to enhance spiritually. We have been created in the image and likeness of God, and we are meant to grow in our spiritual hearing ability; we have been designed to listen for His voice and to comprehend what He is saying.

Our lives belong to God entirely. Just like the Holy Spirit, you and I do not originate kingdom decisions or initiate kingdom actions. We respond. We obey. We follow. We keep listening for His voice the whole time.

We must be intentional about learning to hear in a spiritual sense—and sustained in that intention. I learned this the hard way. Years ago,

I felt overwhelmed by the amount of revelatory truth I was learning. I was not able to put it all into action in my life because it just seemed like too much to deal with. But instead of asking the Lord to help me process everything, I blurted out to Him in frustration, "Lord, I don't think I can take anything more. I just can't hear any more new truths until I have learned to walk in the ones You have already showed me."

Well, guess what? The Lord decided to answer that prayer, and for a whole year I did not hear anything fresh or new from the Holy Spirit. On my own initiative, I had privately placed a low ceiling over myself. Out of weariness and frustration, I had stated that I didn't want to listen anymore; and even though I had done it without thinking, the Lord listened to my request and withdrew.

As that year went by, I felt I was groping in the dark for His guidance. I began to realize that I had erected some kind of a barrier between us, but I had no clue what it could be. Then one particular day I went out for a stroll, praying as I walked. Suddenly, I "heard" (in my spirit) the voice of the Holy Spirit! He said, *You're searching, aren't you?*

I said, "Yeah."

You aren't going to find it, He replied. I did not know how to respond to that. I know I felt within that familiar sense of frustration, and I was thinking, *Why do You always have to speak in parables?*

Then He explained: *You are looking for your own life, but you cannot find it. That is because you gave it to Me. Your life is hidden in Christ now, remember? And once you give your life to Me, I keep it.* That rang true. I was now eager to rescind my mistaken request. What had I been thinking last year? My life was not my own anymore. My new life was hidden in Christ, and it must be revealed to me in an ongoing way—by its Owner.

HUNGRY FOR GOD

In His loving wisdom, God let me be hungry so that I would want to eat only what He would provide. The Holy Spirit had not abandoned me; Papa God was taking care of me!

I fell in love with these words from the book of Deuteronomy:

He humbled you, causing you to hunger and then feeding you with manna, which neither you nor your ancestors had known, to teach you that man does not live on bread alone but on every word that comes from the mouth of the LORD. (Deuteronomy 8:3)

I know that Jesus loved those words, too, because He quoted the last part of that verse in His Sermon on the Mount: *"It is written, 'Man shall not live by bread alone, but by every word that proceeds from the mouth of God'"* (Matthew 4:4 NKJV). In the New Testament Greek, the tense of the word *"proceeds"* indicates an ongoing process. In other words, it means the word that has come, the word that does come, and the word that will come. Where does the word come from? *"The mouth of God."*

God's word is our daily bread. Even Jesus's model prayer (which we call the Lord's Prayer) has this line in it: *"Give us this day our daily bread"* (Matthew 6:11 KJV, NKJV). More than a bakery loaf is implied here. Every bit as important as physical food for our bodies is the spiritual food that comes from God, and we receive that kind of food through our spiritual hearing. We walk with God in a close relationship, and His Spirit speaks truth to our spirits.

Our receptivity to God's truth includes four underlying components: (1) humility, (2) hunger, (3) being fed, and (4) understanding the truth. All of these elements can be found in the above verse from Deuteronomy. It talks about how God humbled the Israelites, which is what He did with me during that long year when I felt far from Him. Yet we can humble ourselves, too. That is what Peter advised the believers to do: *"Humble yourselves under the mighty hand of God, that He may exalt you in due time"* (1 Peter 5:6 NKJV).

In my experience, humility and hunger go hand in hand; and without the humble desire for a word from God, we will not be satisfied. You might even call this kind of hunger a gift from God. He gives us hunger for Him—especially when we ask for it. Too many people are not hungry and thirsty for God, and as a result they do not encounter Him.

I pray, "Lord, make me hungry for more of You. Make me as thirsty as the deer who pants for the brook of water. Make my soul yearn for You." (See Psalm 42:1.) He hears that prayer, and He makes me hungry and thirsty for whatever He desires to feed me. I know He will choose the perfect word for me and will open my heart to understand it.

> OUR RECEPTIVITY TO GOD'S TRUTH INVOLVES HUMILITY, HUNGER, BEING FED, AND UNDERSTANDING THE TRUTH.

IT TAKES TWO TO COMMUNICATE

It is not that we don't recognize God's voice—most of the time, anyway. It is that so many of our prayers are requests, and in the midst of our self-concerned recitation of needs, it seldom occurs to us to stop and listen for the voice of God's Spirit. If we do, we will learn to hear. Jesus said, *"My sheep hear My voice, and I know them, and they follow Me"* (John 10:27 NKJV). I could say so much about that remarkable statement. In this context, I will highlight the simple fact that our capacity to follow Jesus corresponds to our ability to hear His voice— and our attention to it. When we hear His word, we can follow.

Jesus will summon us and even invite Himself into our hearts, but we must assent. Here is how He pictures it for us: *"Behold, I stand at the door and knock. If anyone hears My voice and opens the door, I will come in to him and dine with him, and he with Me"* (Revelation 3:20 NKJV). The first person of the Godhead that you will meet and experience is the Holy Spirit, because when He speaks, He makes Jesus and the Father a living reality for us. He convicts us of our need for Him. People do not even know they need to be saved until the Spirit knocks on the door of their hearts. But once He knocks on someone's heart, it is up to the person to open the door. Jesus did not say He would open the door of each person's heart, only that He would knock on the door. What does He do? He initiates what is meant to be a two-way relationship: "*I will come in to him and dine with him, and he with Me.*" The fellowship is real, but it depends upon the person's response to Jesus's invitation.

As we learn to listen in our conversations with Him, He will share His heart with us. Again, we cannot dominate the conversation by talking only about our problems. He is after a real relationship, not a mere business transaction. And when He sends us out to do something, He sends us as His friend, not as a faceless messenger.

Our relationship with our heavenly Papa was never meant to be a long-distance telephone conversation. "Available" is God's middle name. He yearns to spend time alone with each one of us; and He listens attentively, showing us how to listen to Him. Pastor Dutch Sheets, intercessory leader and revivalist, asks this probing question: "What topic could possibly deserve more of our attention than listening to God? When the source of all life and wisdom speaks, those who would be wise listen. The foolish either don't care to or don't learn how. The fruit of both is the same: destructive ignorance."[10]

Listening is just as important in our closest human relationships, isn't it? When my family was young and I needed to travel and be away from my wife and children for a time, I would use my mobile phone, another telephone, or any other available technology to keep in touch with them. But what we really needed was to touch each other, see each other, and hear each other speak in person. True love requires being together. Sometimes I just need a hug. Similarly, the greatest secret to hearing God's voice is cultivating a love-based, two-way relationship with Him.

In my book *Hearing God's Voice Today*, I highlighted this significant truth: "God's loving desire to be in communication with us never

---

10. Dutch Sheets, foreword to *Listen, God Is Speaking to You*, by Quin Sherrer (Ann Arbor, MI: Servant Publications, 1999), 9.

HEARING: "WHATEVER HE HEARS, HE WILL SPEAK" 61

ebbs or ceases.... We are the ones who must lean into His heart to hear His sweet love language."[11] Our loving Father is speaking. Are we listening?

> THE GREATEST SECRET TO
> HEARING GOD'S VOICE IS
> CULTIVATING A LOVE-BASED,
> TWO-WAY RELATIONSHIP WITH HIM.

HOW DOES GOD EXPRESS HIMSELF?

God does not speak in the same way each time. In fact, He uses quite a range of ways to express Himself, not only the classic "thundering" or "trumpet blast" from heaven, such as we see in some Scripture passages:

I was in the Spirit on the Lord's day, and I heard behind me a loud voice like the sound of a trumpet. (Revelation 1:10 NASB)

His feet were like bronze glowing in a furnace, and his voice was like the sound of rushing waters. (Revelation 1:15)

The voice of the LORD is over the waters; the God of glory thunders; the LORD is over many waters. The voice of the LORD is powerful; the voice of the LORD is full of majesty. The voice of the LORD breaks the cedars, yes, the LORD splinters the cedars of Lebanon.... The voice of the LORD divides the flames of fire. The voice of the LORD shakes the wilderness; the LORD shakes the Wilderness of Kadesh. The voice of the LORD makes the deer give birth, and strips the forests bare; and in His temple everyone says, "Glory!" (Psalm 29:3–5, 7–9 NKJV)

---

11. James W. Goll, *Hearing God's Voice Today* (Grand Rapids, MI: Chosen Books, 2016), 61.

Although God's voice can come in the form of strong, powerful sounds that are not human speech, such as thunder, rushing wind, crashing waves, or earthquakes, this is not always the case. The prophet Elijah discovered this when he could not detect the voice of the Lord in loud natural sounds but rather in a small, whispery breeze:

> The LORD said, "Go out and stand on the mountain in the presence of the LORD, for the LORD is about to pass by." Then a great and powerful wind tore the mountains apart and shattered the rocks before the LORD, but the LORD was not in the wind. After the wind there was an earthquake, but the LORD was not in the earthquake. After the earthquake came a fire, but the LORD was not in the fire. And after the fire came a gentle whisper. When Elijah heard it, he pulled his cloak over his face and went out and stood at the mouth of the cave.   (1 Kings 19:11–13)

Sometimes God speaks to us in what sounds like human speech to our natural ears, and it arrests our attention. That is certainly what happened to Paul on the road to Damascus:

> As he journeyed he came near Damascus, and suddenly a light shone around him from heaven. Then he fell to the ground, and heard a voice saying to him, "Saul, Saul, why are you persecuting Me?" And he said, "Who are You, Lord?" Then the Lord said, "I am Jesus, whom you are persecuting. It is hard for you to kick against the goads." So he, trembling and astonished, said, "Lord, what do You want me to do?" Then the Lord said to him, "Arise and go into the city, and you will be told what you must do." And the men who journeyed with him stood speechless, hearing a voice but seeing no one.   (Acts 9:3–7 NKJV)

There are times when God speaks through His angelic messengers. The most striking example of this occurred when the angel Gabriel announced to Mary that she was going to conceive and bear the Son of God:

> God sent the angel Gabriel to Nazareth, a town in Galilee, to a virgin pledged to be married to a man named Joseph, a descendant

of David. The virgin's name was Mary. The angel went to her and said, "Greetings, you who are highly favored! The Lord is with you." Mary was greatly troubled at his words and wondered what kind of greeting this might be. But the angel said to her, "Do not be afraid, Mary; you have found favor with God. You will conceive and give birth to a son, and you are to call him Jesus. He will be great and will be called the Son of the Most High. The Lord God will give him the throne of his father David, and he will reign over Jacob's descendants forever; his kingdom will never end." "How will this be," Mary asked the angel, "since I am a virgin?" The angel answered, "The Holy Spirit will come on you, and the power of the Most High will overshadow you. So the holy one to be born will be called the Son of God. Even Elizabeth your relative is going to have a child in her old age, and she who was said to be unable to conceive is in her sixth month. For no word from God will ever fail."   (Luke 1:26–37)

Soon afterward, a different angel spoke to Mary's fiancé, Joseph, but it happened in a dream that time. (See Matthew 1:20–21.) Sometimes when God speaks through dreams, people wake up with His words ringing in their minds, or they understand God's message after they think about how to interpret the symbolism in the dream. Likewise, symbolism in visions must often be interpreted in order to understand God's messages. The Holy Spirit will help us to understand, sometimes by speaking directly to us, as He did with Peter:

About noon…, Peter went up on the roof to pray. He became hungry and wanted something to eat, and while the meal was being prepared, he fell into a trance. He saw heaven opened and something like a large sheet being let down to earth by its four corners. It contained all kinds of four-footed animals, as well as reptiles and birds. Then a voice told him, "Get up, Peter. Kill and eat." "Surely not, Lord!" Peter replied. "I have never eaten anything impure or unclean." The voice spoke to him a second time, "Do not call anything impure that God has made clean." This happened three times, and immediately the sheet was taken back to heaven. While

Peter was wondering about the meaning of the vision, the men sent by Cornelius found out where Simon's house was and stopped at the gate. They called out, asking if Simon who was known as Peter was staying there. While Peter was still thinking about the vision, the Spirit said to him, "Simon, three men are looking for you. So get up and go downstairs. Do not hesitate to go with them, for I have sent them." Peter went down and said to the men, "I'm the one you're looking for. Why have you come?" (Acts 10:9–21)

Often, however, God's voice is inaudible, yet we can "hear" it within our quiet spirits. As His sheep, we recognize the voice as His.

The fact is, the more we release the sounds of heaven on earth through our faithful and fervent praise and worship, the more frequently and clearly we will hear the voice of the Lord. And the more we hear His voice, the better we can bring His glory to earth and encourage other people. We see in the following messianic prophecy from Isaiah that hearing from God enables His disciples to speak for Him widely:

The Lord GOD has given Me the tongue of the learned, that I should know how to speak a word in season to him who is weary. He awakens Me morning by morning, He awakens My ear to hear as the learned. The Lord GOD has opened My ear; and I was not rebellious, nor did I turn away. (Isaiah 50:4–5 NKJV)

The word of the Lord is powerful, but it will never overrule a person's response to it; thus we have this warning:

But encourage one another daily, as long as it is called "Today," so that none of you may be hardened by sin's deceitfulness.... "Today, if you hear his voice, do not harden your hearts...."
(Hebrews 3:13, 15)

"But encourage one another daily." This phrase points to one of the primary purposes of hearing God's voice—extending His fatherly love to other people. Through our relationship with Him, we can help extend His invitation to those who otherwise might not know Him.

"Come to Me," Jesus says, *"all you who labor and are heavy laden, and I will give you rest. Take My yoke upon you and learn from Me, for I am gentle and lowly in heart, and you will find rest for your souls"* (Matthew 11:28–29 NKJV).

LEARN TO RECOGNIZE HIS VOICE

When you are in doubt about what you think you may be hearing from the Lord, you can run it through the following guidelines to test it. Even when God issues a strong or startling word, you can count on it to line up with His merciful character. Note these important points:

1. God leads you. Evil pushes you.

2. God stills you. Evil rushes you.

3. God reassures you. Evil frightens you.

4. God enlightens you. Evil confuses you.

5. God encourages you. Evil discourages you.

6. God comforts you. Evil worries you.

7. God calms you. Evil agitates you.

8. God convicts you (of the truth). Evil condemns you.

> CHECK WHAT YOU THINK
> YOU ARE HEARING AGAINST
> THE WRITTEN WORD OF GOD,
> BECAUSE GOD WILL NEVER
> CONTRADICT HIMSELF.

Check what you think you are hearing against the written Word of God, because God will never contradict Himself. Before you share any word with others, pay attention to the fruit the word is bearing in your own heart. Does it bring you hope? Do you feel a surge of courage or faith? Or does it seem to accuse you or engender ungodly fear within you? Remember that Satan and God are in conflict, and the devil would like nothing better than to drive you away from the Lord, your Source of life. The enemy *"prowls around like a roaring lion looking for someone to devour. Resist him"* (1 Peter 5:8–9).

So ask yourself whether a word you feel you have received resonates with your spirit. When you hear a true word from God, you can expect to experience what is called the "witness of the Holy Spirit." Remember, counterfeit words will leave you feeling anxious or agitated or even angry.

GENTLE AND LOWLY

As we look for the best way to position ourselves to hear and obey God's voice, Jesus is our model. Our Lord and Savior and Friend epitomizes power under control. He does not need to speak with the strength of a nuclear explosion. In the above passage from Matthew, He refers to Himself as *"gentle and lowly"* (Matthew 11:29 nkjv).

When we are young, many of us want to be powerful, rich, and famous. We cannot see the value of humble service. However, God speaks more clearly to those who lower themselves willingly. I grasped this fact years ago when I was traveling with the healing evangelist Mahesh Chavda, serving as his assistant.

On one occasion, we were in the Czech city of Prague, and he was praying individually with hundreds of people who had stayed after the evening service. He was so completely occupied with praying that he could not take a break. In the wee hours of the morning, I made my way back to our hotel room to fetch a couple of things: his tennis shoes and a carafe of coffee. I brought them back to the place where he was still patiently praying for people, although he was exhausted. He was wearing his black dress shoes, as he always did when he preached. I knelt down next to him and untied his shoes, slipped them off one at a time, and slid his feet into his more comfortable tennis shoes. Then I gave him the coffee to help restore his energy.

It was such a simple thing, and yet so powerful. I was not in that relationship for what I might be able to get out of it, but really in order to serve in whatever way I could. And I gleaned so much from watching him and talking with him. Our relationship (which has now lasted more than forty years) was good.

On another occasion, I remember asking Mahesh, "Now that you have been walking with God for these many years, and you have seen miracles and healings and have fasted and prayed, tell me what you have learned about hearing the voice of God."

I thought he might reply, "First you need to fast for forty days and forty nights, and then you need to give away all you own." Only then, perhaps, would God's voice be able to penetrate a person's feeble comprehension. Presumably, God would send a multitude of angels to clear the way for His booming announcement.

But Mahesh just smiled and said, "The closer I get to God, the more gentle His voice becomes to me."

That is all.

You see, it is all about the relationship.

REACHING FOR A HIGHER REALM

In thinking about our relationship with the Lord and hearing His voice, one of my favorite hymns from childhood comes to mind. The words go like this:

I come to the garden alone
While the dew is still on the roses,
And the voice I hear falling on my ear,
The Son of God discloses.
    Refrain:
    And he walks with me, and he talks with me,
    And he tells me I am his own;
    And the joy we share as we tarry there,
    None other has ever known.[12]

---

12. C. Austin Miles, "I Come to the Garden Alone," 1912.

I have sung this song for over fifty years. It means as much to me today as when I first sang it from my burgundy-brown Cokesbury hymnal. Yes, there is such joy in hearing the voice of God. It does not matter what He chooses to say. Simply because it is *He*, our hearts leap up. We lay down whatever may have distracted our attention from Him and hasten to do whatever He tells us to do.

Yet many of us still harbor unbelief with regard to the idea of hearing God's voice. We lack confidence that it is really possible, and we just cannot grasp the fact that He loves us and invites us to sit with Him. Some of us have had bad experiences of mistakenly thinking we heard God's voice, and we are afraid that we will make another error or be deceived; as a result, we have decided to take the safe path of not opening ourselves up at all to hear God.

Let's remember that the Creator of all things created communication, too. He is infinitely capable of speaking to you in a manner that you can receive. He knows you better than anybody else, and He wants to speak to you in a way that you can understand. Do not wait until you are desperate to hear His voice. Activate your spiritual hearing by asking Him questions and expecting answers. You may be surprised when fresh thoughts begin to flow through your mind. He *will* answer you somehow—through another person's testimony or teaching, in a line or two from His written Word, by means of a dream, or another way. Let Him decide how to speak. Just listen expectantly.[13]

GOD KNOWS YOU BETTER
THAN ANYBODY ELSE,
AND HE WANTS TO SPEAK TO YOU
IN A WAY THAT YOU CAN UNDERSTAND.

---

13. For a more in-depth study on this topic, refer to my book *Hearing God's Voice Today*. See footnote 11.

PRAYER OF A DISCERNING HEART

Gracious Father, in Jesus's wonderful name, I present both my physical and spiritual ears to You. I want to be a modern-day disciple like John the Beloved, leaning my head upon Your chest so that I can hear Your very heartbeat. According to Your Word, I ask that You would open my ears every morning to hear Your life-giving words. Fine-tune my discernment so that I can tell Your voice from others' and so that I can distinguish it even when You speak in unusual and unexpected ways.

Awaken my weary heart to hear Your voice. I want to hear Your inspiring and convicting voice for my own sake and for the sake of others. I want to be more effective for Your purposes. I ask outright for an increase of Your anointing on the gift of hearing Your voice. Give me the grace I need to pursue You and to keep listening for Your voice all the days of my life. With gratitude, I praise Your name. Amen.

4

FEELING:
"FROM THE HEART FLOW
THE ISSUES OF LIFE"

"Watch over your heart with all diligence, for from it flow the springs ["issues" KJV, NKJV] of life."
—Proverbs 4:23 (NASB)

W e have examined seeing and hearing—two of the all-important human senses that are part of our physical composition—as well as their spiritual implications. All of our five basic physical senses (sight, hearing, touch, taste, and smell) are also essential to our spiritual makeup, because they function to receive and discern revelation from God.

Let us now turn to the spiritual equivalent of the physical sense of touch, which is *feeling,* as in our feelings or emotional responses to the environment around us. In this chapter, we will explore the question of how our feelings help us to pick up spiritual information. To begin, consider the fact that people who are blind or deaf, even partially, rely much more heavily on their remaining senses. For example, if you were unable to see the words and sentences in this book, you would be grateful for a braille or audio-format book. Similarly, you can think of your feelings as a sort of emotional/

spiritual braille-reader—a way you can pick up on the signals that your other senses may miss.

For years, we have heard the saying "WWJD (What Would Jesus Do?)" I want to propose an additional question: "WWJF (What Would Jesus Feel?)" In my observation, many of the men and women whom God assigns to be prophets or intercessors are people whose hearts are more sensitive than others. Sometimes they can tell what the Spirit is doing not only because they can detect subtle shifts in the spiritual atmosphere, but also because they can feel actual physical pain or other sensations. For instance, that is what is happening in a public meeting when healing prayer is called for on someone's behalf because a prayer warrior notices a foreign pain or numbness or tingling in a part of his or her own body.

THIS GETS PERSONAL

Personal sensitivity is usually thought of as a feminine trait, but I happen to be one of those rare males for whom feelings are paramount; I am a "sensitive male." I am emotionally wired, as anybody who spends time with me knows. People like me have been created in God's image with a little extra emphasis on the feeling factor, and I want to be as sensitive as I can be when it comes to discerning the desires of the Lord's heart. I have had to continually learn how to surrender my "feelers" to the Holy Spirit so that God can use me in the way that He intended when He created me this way.

One of my life goals is to become even more sensitive—to the Holy Spirit. I want to be sensitive to His nudges, to His embraces, to the nuances of His working, to His backing off. I want to know as much as possible about what draws Him, what invites Him to come in, and what dissuades Him from staying. After all, as R. T. Kendall points out so well in his book *The Sensitivity of the Spirit*, the Holy Spirit Himself is sensitive, like a dove.

Over the years, I have had to learn how to stay sensitive to the Holy Spirit without becoming overreactive. I discovered that I had certain prejudices I did not realize I had. Particular memories were correlated with stored emotions. When something triggered those memories, out spilled my old feelings, and they were rarely useful in my immediate context. Such reactions had a lot to do with the condition of my heart, my inner being. I have received personal ministry and learned a lot in the process. Where I have suffered from negative experiences, even traumas, I have sought inner healing. Essential to my increasing wholeness has been a healthy sense of personal value, based on the fact that I am *"accepted in the beloved"* (Ephesians 1:6 KJV, NKJV). Unhealed hurts can make us insecure, inhibited, imprudent, anxious, irritable, or combative—nothing like the fruit of the Spirit that we want to harvest. I am making it my goal to respond with God's love to everything that touches my feelings, out of a heart that is as healed and whole as possible.

WHAT FLOWS FROM YOUR HEART?

Thus, what flows out of our hearts affects everything in and around us. That is the reason I chose Proverbs 4:23 as the initial Scripture for this chapter: *"Watch over your heart with all diligence, for from it flow the springs* ["issues" KJV, NKJV] *of life."* Whether or not you identify yourself as a feeler-type of person, the state of your heart, your inner being, either muddies your life-spring or clarifies its flow. Therefore, you must scrutinize (*"watch over"*) your motives, your assumptions, and the fruit of your actions.

The only way you can truly understand yourself is to measure what flows from your heart against Scripture. I can think of at least five aspects to a foundational understanding of our emotional makeup:

1. The heart-hardening effect of sin. Hebrews 3:13 talks about how our hearts can become hardened by *"sin's deceitfulness."* The same Holy Spirit who convicts us of sin at the beginning of our Christian life will continually help us to identify sins in our lives and to repent of them; He leads us in progressive sanctification. Nobody will be completely perfected in this earthly life, but as a result of the cleansing work of God's Spirit, we can expect our hearts to grow into heavenly health.

2. *The only way to soften a hard heart.* You can best counter the heart-hardening effect of sin by breaking it with God's hammer—His Word. "'*Is not my word like fire,*' declares the LORD, '*and like a hammer that breaks a rock in pieces?*'" (Jeremiah 23:29). Specific scriptural words shatter specific kinds of hardness; you can pray that God will bring them to your attention at the right times.

3. *The desires of our heart.* "*Do not love the world or the things in the world*" (1 John 2:15 NKJV), wrote the apostle John. He was echoing Jesus, who taught us not to lay up treasures on earth but to lay up treasures in heaven, concluding, "*For where your treasure is, there your heart will be also*" (Matthew 6:21 NKJV; see verses 19–20). These days, people are fond of saying, "Follow your passion," but do not follow your passions and desires if it means that your love for worldly things outstrips your love for God. Rather, aim to "*delight yourself in the LORD; and He will give you the desires of your heart*" (Psalm 37:4 NASB).

4. *Heart-fixing hope.* Lest all this talk of hard-heartedness and repentance discourage you, let me quickly add that the Lord is always available for you, always loving you. Fix your attention on Him. "*Everyone who has this hope fixed on Him purifies himself, just as He is pure*" (1 John 3:3 NASB). In other words, fixing your hope on Him fixes your heart.

5. *Pure-hearted love, true-hearted godliness.* In order to experience the redemption of our feelings, we must present them to God on a regular basis. *We* must present them, while eliminating the polluting influences that we are so fond of. Paul wrote, "*Dear friends, let us purify ourselves from everything that contaminates body and spirit, perfecting holiness out of reverence for God*" (2 Corinthians 7:1). And we have the assurance that "*if we confess our sins, He is faithful and just to forgive us our sins and to cleanse us from all unrighteousness*" (1 John 1:9 NKJV).

I recommend setting aside a special time annually for a personal heart checkup. Pray over the condition of your heart and immerse yourself in the Word. Ask for restoration and renewal, praying, "*Create in me a clean heart, O God, and renew a steadfast spirit within me*" (Psalm 51:10 NKJV).

If you end up wrestling over and over with the same unwanted emotional response, you might need to seek help from someone who ministers out of an integrated healing model that combines prayer counseling, inner healing, deliverance, and insightful feedback. Ask the Lord to show you what to do when you feel stuck.

> THE STATE OF YOUR HEART,
> YOUR INNER BEING,
> EITHER MUDDIES YOUR
> LIFE-SPRING OR CLARIFIES ITS FLOW.

DEMONSTRATING GOD'S COMPASSION

A powerful aspect of our spiritual sense of touch is the response of compassion. I want you to know something: "compassion" is not meek and mild—it is volcanic! When compassion surges up in your heart, it propels you out of your self-concern. You reach out, ignoring the personal cost, to do whatever you can for another person.

The compassion in our hearts that is prompted by God's Spirit matches the compassionate heart of Jesus. Here are some scriptural glimpses of His compassion in action:

When He saw the multitudes, He was moved with compassion for them, because they were weary and scattered, like sheep having no shepherd. (Matthew 9:36 NKJV)

Moved with compassion, Jesus stretched out His hand and touched him, and said to him, "I am willing; be cleansed." (Mark 1:41 NASB)

Jesus called His disciples to Him, and said, "I feel compassion for the people, because they have remained with Me now three days and have nothing to eat; and I do not want to send them away hungry, for they might faint on the way."

(Matthew 15:32 NASB)

When the Lord saw her, He felt compassion for her, and said to her, "Do not weep."

(Luke 7:13 NASB)

Jesus continued [telling parables, saying,]: "...So he got up and went to his father. But while he was still a long way off, his father saw him and was filled with compassion for him; he ran to his son, threw his arms around him and kissed him." (Luke 15:11, 20)

The deep needs of the people around Him drew a compassionate response from Jesus. This often happened without words, as it did with the woman who had the issue of blood:

Now a certain woman had a flow of blood for twelve years, and had suffered many things from many physicians. She had spent all that she had and was no better, but rather grew worse. When she heard about Jesus, she came behind Him in the crowd and touched His garment. For she said, "If only I may touch His clothes, I shall be made well." Immediately the fountain of her blood was dried up, and she felt in her body that she was healed of the affliction. And Jesus, immediately knowing in Himself that power had gone out of Him, turned around in the crowd and said, "Who touched My clothes?" But His disciples said to Him, "You see the multitude thronging You, and You say, 'Who touched Me?'" And He looked around to see her who had done this thing. But the woman, fearing and trembling, knowing what had happened to her, came and fell down before Him and told Him the whole truth. And He said to her, "Daughter, your faith has made you well. Go in peace, and be healed of your affliction." (Mark 5:25–34 NKJV)

Talk about Jesus being spiritually and emotionally sensitive! The woman did not say a single word. She did not even touch Jesus's body in any way that He could have felt; she touched only the hem of His clothing, and yet He could tell that something significant had transpired. His disciples had never encountered such a situation. "What do you mean, 'Someone touched Me?' Everybody in this crowd is touching You!" They did not know that He could *feel* power going out of Himself to meet a desperate, unspecified need. He felt both the compassion and the surge of divine power that met that unspoken need. Jesus's loving heart continually went out to the people, who were like sheep without a shepherd. His authority over disease and darkness were so solidly rooted in His compassionate heart that the enemy (who suffers from a serious lack of compassion) could not remain in His presence. As John Wimber used to say, "Everything God does is related to who He is." When Jesus walked the earth, He healed the sick and searched tirelessly for God's lost sheep. Today, because Jesus's Spirit dwells in each of us, we should, too.

The best Christian leaders exemplify Jesus's loving compassion on a daily basis. Take Mahesh Chavda, for example, whose first book is called (tellingly), *Only Love Can Make a Miracle*. And I recall Heidi Baker's often-repeated words, "You must learn to stop for the one," referring to the way we must treat anybody—even the lowliest person—whose needs come to our attention.

I also remember what Oral Roberts, that venerable general of the faith, said just before he died, a story I also included in my book *Releasing Spiritual Gifts Today*. My son Justin and I were invited, along with some others, to visit the healing evangelist. Each person was allowed to ask one question or make one comment, and then we could ask Oral Roberts to pray for us. Justin's request was bold: "I want greater authority and effectiveness in my praying for the sick."

Oral Roberts looked at him and said, "Son, you don't know what you're asking for."

Justin repeated his request anyway. "That's what I want from God: greater authority and effectiveness when I pray for the sick."

Then Oral Roberts said something I had never heard anyone say before: "For that, you must learn to love the sick." The words of this renowned evangelist resonated in the room, and I knew we had just heard a major kingdom secret: "You must learn to love the sick."

Compassion again. We must learn to love the often unlovable people we reach out to. We must hold the compassion of Jesus's Spirit in the highest esteem and stir it up in our hearts. Far from being timid or boring, compassion is one powerful *feeling* that covers a lot of ground in the kingdom of God!

COMPASSION IS NOT MEEK AND MILD—
IT IS VOLCANIC!

GOD'S HEART IN OURS

The Scriptures tell us that Jesus came from the bosom (heart) of the Father (see John 1:18 KJV, NKJV) and that now, by faith, He resides in the hearts of those who love Him: "*The mystery that has been kept hidden for ages and generations…is now disclosed to the Lord's people. To them God has chosen to make known among the Gentiles the glorious riches of this mystery, which is Christ in you, the hope of glory*" (Colossians 1:26–27). Consequently, Christians are called temples of the Holy Spirit. (See 1 Corinthians 3:16; 6:19.)

For our whole lives, each of us can expect to have repeated Emmaus-road experiences in which our spirits interact with God's Spirit within. (See Luke 24:13–35.) Initiation and response; initiation and response. Your heart will not always burn as the disciples' hearts did on the road to Emmaus, but you can expect your emotions to detect spiritual activity and spiritual atmosphere on a regular basis.

Stay alert for those subtle nudges and fleeting ideas that just might be important. Keep a silent dialogue going with the Spirit during the course of your daily walk. He never leaves you; He dwells in your heart.

PROPHETIC INTERCESSION

As part of their spiritual sense of touch, many people feel the weighty pressure of others' burdensome problems. Paul wrote, "*Bear one another's burdens, and thereby fulfill the law of Christ"* (Galatians 6:2 NASB). He was not talking about lugging heavy backpacks. Fulfilling the law of Christ is a heart thing.

For sure, the most difficult part of any burdensome issue is the internal effect. The only way we can truly bear someone else's burden is to shoulder some of the emotional and spiritual weight. Sometimes we can do that by sharing something from God's Word, but the most effective way to bear one another's burdens is to pray.

We do not know how to pray for each new burden that presents itself. We cannot expect other people to tell us how to pray, either. The Holy Spirit, however, knows all the ins and outs of every matter. He knows how a crisis fits in with the divine plan. He knows all about human fears and foibles. Thus, the only way to *"bear one another's burdens, and thereby fulfill the law of Christ"* is to move through life with an intimate awareness of the Spirit and His guidance.

I have a name for this burden-bearing: I call it "prophetic intercession," and I have written and taught about it in great detail.[14] Prophetic intercessors are like willing little beasts of burden that Jesus can ride on. Prophetic intercessors get to carry Him from assignment to assignment. The burdens we carry in prayer are not meant to crush us or consume us. None of them are permanent, although many are repeated. We are supposed to carry the burden somewhere, but we are not supposed to keep it. Our job is to deliver it to the throne of grace: *"Let us therefore come boldly to the throne of grace, that we may obtain mercy and find grace to help in time of need"* (Hebrews 4:16 NKJV).

Sometimes it is my job to carry a burden for only a short while. Other times, the journey is longer. Often, I feel called to bless someone else who is carrying a burden, without carrying it myself. But I have found that I am not supposed to even touch some things. Without the gift of discernment and a continual flow of internal communication with the Holy Spirit, I could not tell which burden was which. And without the compassionate love of Christ, I cannot pray suitably.

---

14. See, for example, my book *The Prophetic Intercessor* (Grand Rapids, MI: Chosen Books, 2007).

It seems to be the case that some people are wired to carry a prayer burden for longer periods of time than others. All of us should be alert to the idea that our assignment may consist of only a small piece of the bigger burden. For example, when praying for a national election, my contribution might be to pray only for one local individual. In any case, I must develop a sensitivity to the Holy Spirit that will enable me to gauge the type of praying I am supposed to do.

> THE ONLY WAY TO *"BEAR ONE ANOTHER'S BURDENS"* IS TO MOVE THROUGH LIFE WITH AN INTIMATE AWARENESS OF THE SPIRIT AND HIS GUIDANCE.

I must maintain a trusting, worshipful attitude at all times. This is the Father's business, and I am honored to be invited to participate in it. In fact, I am yoked with the Lord. As a co-laborer in the harvest field, I go where He goes, starting and stopping as He does. I am not in charge, and I am not pulling 100 percent of the weight. Jesus says, *"For my yoke is easy and my burden is light"* (Matthew 11:30). All a beast of burden needs is a willing and obedient heart.

As I move ahead, yoked with the Lord, He signals His intentions by means of subtle shifts and movements. In order to keep pace, I must be sensitive to feelings of pressure and release. Only rarely will words be spoken. When I encounter encumbrances or obstacles, I need to know quickly what to do.

Walking by faith by means of my Holy-Spirit-yoked spirit, I also need to discern the spiritual atmosphere around me. Is it friendly or unfriendly? Did I just feel something shift? Is that extra pressure I feel coming from the Holy Spirit or from a demonic spirit? Is my own tendency to drag my feet (or another faulty tendency) interfering with my keeping a steady pace? In other words, am I feeling something that comes from God, from Satan, or from my own flesh?

In the process of discerning a situation, I must never lapse into critical judgment, particularly where another person is concerned. Keeping in mind the fruit of the Spirit, I must resist any temptation to grow impatient, frustrated, unpleasant, or hopeless. I will never have to take a situation into my own hands, because God *always* has a solution to every problem.

One goal of my discernment is not so much to escape a predicament as it is to stay close to the Lord and follow His leading. Another goal of mine (and I trust it is yours, as well), is to continue to develop all of my natural and spiritual senses to discern good and evil. I am always learning to pay better attention. I have been mentored in this by the founder of Generals International, Cindy Jacobs, as we have ministered together numerous times. I always tune in when I hear her say, "Something just shifted! Did you feel that?" She is so good at picking up on even atmospheric changes as prophetic intercession and acts of obedience and faith usher in God's manifest presence.

WALKING BY OUR SPIRIT-GUIDED FEELINGS

Sometimes I feel quite limited by the weaknesses of my human frame, but then I remember that even my discernment comes from God. My walk is a walk of faith.

> For we who are in this [earthly] tent [of our human bodies] groan, being burdened, not because we want to be unclothed, but further clothed, that mortality may be swallowed up by life. Now He who has prepared us for this very thing is God, who also has given us the Spirit as a guarantee.... For we walk by faith, not by sight.... Therefore we make it our aim, whether present or absent, to be well pleasing to Him.   (2 Corinthians 5:4–5, 7, 9 NKJV)

I do not walk by my own (very undependable) human feelings, but rather by my Holy-Spirit-guided feelings. The difference is significant, and it begins the moment I present myself to God and yield all of my senses to Him. Paul insists that this is the only way for a mere human being to be able to approach discernment:

> *Therefore, I urge you, brothers and sisters, in view of God's mercy,*
> *to offer your bodies as a living sacrifice, holy and pleasing to God—*
> *this is your true and proper worship. Do not conform to the pat-*
> *tern of this world, but be transformed by the renewing of your*
> *mind. Then you will be able to test and approve what God's will*
> *is—his good, pleasing and perfect will.*   (Romans 12:1–2)

As I walk daily by faith, I find that I can usually sense the dif-ference between good and evil. And whenever I am uncertain about which is presenting itself, all I need to do is review the ABCs of God's ways to see if what I am facing lines up with them. What is the moti-vating spirit behind this thing I am uncertain about? Does my spirit bear witness with the Holy Spirit about it? Does it reflect the nature of God? Do I see love in it? Are gifts of the Spirit in operation? Is this situation bearing good fruit?

If I come up with too many unclear answers or flat-out negatives, I can thank my spiritual sense of touch for showing me that this thing is a fraud or even a threat. You know, it is even OK to feel *annoyed* in your spirit when the enemy is badgering you. We see this in the story of Paul and the slave girl who had the demonic spirit of divination, which we discussed in a previous chapter. Even though her words were true, her motivation came from an unclean spirit, and it was time for somebody to deal with it.

> *Once when we were going to the place of prayer, we were met by a*
> *female slave who had a spirit by which she predicted the future. She*
> *earned a great deal of money for her owners by fortune-telling. She*
> *followed Paul and the rest of us, shouting, "These men are servants*
> *of the Most High God, who are telling you the way to be saved."*
> *She kept this up for many days. Finally Paul became so annoyed*
> *that he turned around and said to the spirit, "In the name of Jesus*
> *Christ I command you to come out of her!" At that moment the*
> *spirit left her.*   (Acts 16:16–18)

This is an example of a disciple whose emotions were being guided by God. Although we may never run into a similar situation, we can learn from it, asking the Holy Spirit to help us discern between good and evil as we exercise our spiritual senses.

REACHING FOR A HIGHER REALM

Bill Gaither's song "He Touched Me" has been sung and recorded by many evangelical and charismatic Christians for over fifty years. The lyrics were inspired when somebody pointed out to Bill the number of times the New Testament depicts Jesus touching people. Clearly, the physical act of His touch was accompanied by emotional/spiritual touching—Jesus's compassion met heartfelt needs, often without words. This is how Jesus healed people and drew them out of evil and into the light of God's kingdom.

"He touched me"—He still touches people today, through believers like you and me. Never hesitate to respond to the invitations of His Spirit, and please do not ignore His warnings or corrections. He has equipped each one of us with hidden senses, and He wants to teach us how to trust them.

Always remember—when you love with the compassion of Jesus, you have His authority to bring hope, healing, and deliverance into troublesome situations. Invite the Holy Spirit to come again and touch you deeply with the love of God.

PRAYER OF A DISCERNING HEART

Father, in Jesus's great name, I surrender my mind, my will, and my emotions to You. I consecrate myself to You, and I choose to watch over my heart so that what comes out of it will flow forth with Your love and benefit others. I give You full permission to shatter any stony places that remain in my heart. Enter into my memories and heal any emotional trauma. Equip me with discernment so that I can lay hold of revelation from You, discard evil, and embrace good. Make my heart burn within me with a knowledge of the truth when I come into Your presence.

I ask You for an increase in the anointing of Your Spirit that rests upon my emotions. Teach me to recognize the signals and flags that You raise through my emotions and feelings. Make my feelings match Yours, and enlarge the capacity of my heart for compassion. Make me sensitive to Your slightest suggestions and quick to obey Your directives.

By Your grace, I *believe*—help me to outgrow my unbelief. Increase my passion for the things of Your kingdom. Infuse my spirit with Yours so that I can love You fully and recognize the desires of Your heart. For the glory of God, amen.

5

TASTING, SMELLING, AND OTHER LEADINGS

*"How sweet are Your words to my taste! Yes, sweeter than honey
to my mouth!"*
—Psalm 119:103 (NASB)

*"Thanks be to God, who always leads us as captives in Christ's
triumphal procession and uses us to spread the aroma of the
knowledge of him everywhere."*
—2 Corinthians 2:14

I have been fascinated with the story of Helen Keller's life ever since
I first heard it. Born in 1880, she survived a serious illness when she
was only a year and a half old that robbed her of both her vision and
her hearing. She learned to communicate with her immediate family
by means of some "home signs," but her prospects for a meaningful life
seemed dim.

Then teacher Anne Sullivan came along. Their story has been
told in books, plays, documentaries, and dramatic films, including
The Miracle Worker movies, which are probably most familiar to
today's audiences. Annie broke through the seemingly insurmountable

barriers of blindness, deafness, and muteness when seven-year-old Helen suddenly grasped the connection between the water that was being pumped over one of her hands and the word W-A-T-E-R that her teacher was spelling with her fingers into the other hand.

At a young age, Helen was introduced to Jesus Christ by the famous Boston preacher Phillips Brooks (who wrote the words to "O Little Town of Bethlehem"). With Annie interpreting, Brooks told the little girl the gospel story. Reportedly, her response was joyful, along the lines of, "I always knew He was there, but I didn't know His name!"[15]

Helen learned to develop her sense of touch to a high level of sensitivity (so that she could "listen" to music via its vibrations, for instance). She also typically got her face close enough to things to sniff or taste them. Using only the senses that she had available, she gathered more information about the world around her than most of us do with all five senses in good working order.

Helen Keller went on to become the first deaf-blind person to earn a college degree. Not only did she learn to read, write, and speak, but she also became a published author and advocate for many social causes. To this day, quotes from Helen Keller such as these are in wide circulation: "I can see, and that is why I can be happy, in what you call the dark, but which to me is golden. I can see a God-made world, not a man-made world." "It is a terrible thing to see and have no vision."

NOT GETTING STUCK ON ONE CHANNEL

I have profiled Helen Keller at the beginning of this chapter because she shows us so clearly how, when a person is deprived of one or two of the natural senses, the other senses can shine.

I recall a day many years ago when I was sitting in a living room across from an older Christian gentleman who looked me over and said, "You're not hearing right now, are you?" He was referring to hearing God's voice prophetically, and he was right. It was as though I was

---

15. See, for example, https://books.google.com/ books?id=NeCN2cVnONYC&pg=PA591&dq=Helen+Keller+didn%27t+ know+His+name.

using a radio that was stuck on one channel—and the volume had been turned down.

I took it to the Lord in prayer: "OK, God, in what other ways could You be speaking to me?" Without becoming frustrated or self-condemning, I began to cultivate a hunger for what I now call "God's WWW" (His will, word, and ways). I discovered that God has different times and seasons for revealing Himself to us. Only some of the time should I expect to see visions or hear heavenly words; I needed to learn to be flexible and to yield my entire self—including all of my senses—to the spiritual communication exchange.

I may not be one of those people who is always out in front when a new thing appears—one who is called an "innovator," "inventor," or "early adopter" in the technical development world, or a "forerunner" in the church. But I know when it is time to learn new truths, approaches, and techniques. I admire people in the church who pave the way for the rest of us, people like Patricia King of XP Ministries. Though I am one her ministry advisers, I probably learn from her as much as, or more than, she does from me. Patricia is a spiritual entrepreneur who doesn't give up when she faces difficult circumstances; instead, she strategizes and implements fresh ways of moving forward to do whatever God wants her to do. Like others who run on ahead of the rest of us, she gets misunderstood and criticized. But that does not slow her down. She is constantly learning and pioneering new concepts, without losing sight of God. If somehow her power of speech were taken away, she would find some other way of communicating, and she would make it exciting. Patricia will never, ever be stuck on one channel.

Let us be inspired by those who have gone before us in developing their spiritual senses as we now explore the avenues of taste and smell.

"TASTE AND SEE"

The Scriptures are filled with allusions to the sense of taste, and very few of them are confined to the physical ability. For example:

O taste and see that the LORD is good; how blessed is the man who takes refuge in Him! (Psalm 34:8 NASB)

Is there injustice on my tongue? Cannot my taste discern the unsavory? (Job 6:30 NKJV)

Like an apple tree among the trees of the woods, so is my beloved among the sons. I sat down in his shade with great delight, and his fruit was sweet to my taste. (Song of Solomon 2:3 NKJV[16])

Then the LORD reached out his hand and touched my mouth and said to me, "I have put my words in your mouth." (Jeremiah 1:9)

"Taste" is another way to refer to discernment, isn't it? Sometimes we taste or discern God's goodness, other times the presence of evil. It is as if our tasting gives us eyes—or ears as in the Jeremiah passage. Often, we not only perceive what God is showing us, but we also spread the news.

You could compare this process to a cooking competition. Television programming is filled with shows in which chefs compete for prizes, and the two primary criteria for judging are—you guessed it—taste and presentation. Taste and see.

> "TASTE" IS ANOTHER WAY
> TO REFER TO DISCERNMENT.

SWEETER THAN HONEY

Taste guides our assessment more than we realize. Some things will "taste" good to you, like the perfectly ripened fruit of the Spirit: *"love, joy, peace, patience, kindness, goodness, faithfulness, gentleness, self-control"* (Galatians 5:22–23 NASB). At least two men in the Bible,

---

16. The biblical book from which this verse comes is entitled either "Song of Solomon" or "Song of Songs" depending on the Bible translation.

Ezekiel and John, were commanded to consume scrolls on which the word of God was written, and those scrolls tasted good to them:

> *And he said to me, "Son of man, eat what is before you, eat this scroll; then go and speak to the people of Israel." So I opened my mouth, and he gave me the scroll to eat. Then he said to me, "Son of man, eat this scroll I am giving you and fill your stomach with it." So I ate it, and it tasted as sweet as honey in my mouth.*
>
> (Ezekiel 3:1–3)

> *So I went to the angel and asked him to give me the little scroll. He said to me, "Take it and eat it. It will turn your stomach sour, but 'in your mouth it will be as sweet as honey.'" I took the little scroll from the angel's hand and ate it. It tasted as sweet as honey in my mouth, but when I had eaten it, my stomach turned sour. Then I was told, "You must prophesy again about many peoples, nations, languages and kings."* (Revelation 10:9–11)

LEAVING A BAD TASTE

Other things will seem to leave a bad taste in your mouth. You can't figure it out instantly, but you discern that something is "off," something is rotten. You can almost taste and smell it. That is when your natural senses have come under the anointing of the Holy Spirit, and things have shifted into the supernatural dimension. Or, it might be the gift of distinguishing (or discerning) of spirits in operation (see 1 Corinthians 12:10), which I describe in detail in my book *Releasing Spiritual Gifts Today*.

When this happens, be careful not to jump into action—or reaction—too fast. Sometimes our perception is skewed. Unhealed interior wounds, unrepented-of sin, or faulty instruction can make us suspect a problem that does not exist. Perhaps you are picking up on a real issue, but it is not yet time to do anything more about it. We need to look at things from as many perspectives as possible. Maybe when you got a taste or a whiff of bad fruit, its origin was a generational curse or a demonic spirit of darkness.

Our top two responses when dealing with subjective revelation should always be: (1) presenting our perceived revelation back to God in prayer, asking for confirmation, and (2) inquiring of the Lord for wisdom regarding how and when to apply the revelation.

AROMATIC IMPLICATIONS

THE FRAGRANCE OF HEAVEN

Taste and smell are closely associated with one another, and as we exercise our senses, we can also derive significance from what certain scents and odors symbolize. For example, I was once ministering in some tent meetings in Sacramento, California. Using the book of Leviticus, I was teaching about the sacrificial fire on the altar of the tabernacle: *"Fire shall be kept burning continually on the altar; it is not to go out"* (Leviticus 6:13 NASB). Suddenly the distinct smell of hickory smoke moved forward from the back of the tent. Hundreds of people sniffed at the air. Nobody could see a fire, and there was no altar. Yet with the smell of this invisible smoke, the fear of the Lord came over the place. Leaders spilled out into the aisles and came crawling up to the front in repentance, seeking the face of God. The scent had been the trigger for the people's response.

Another example of a significant scent can be noted in the Bible where, after the flood, Noah made a sacrificial fire on an altar he had built:

> Then Noah built an altar to the LORD and, taking some of all
> the clean animals and clean birds, he sacrificed burnt offerings on
> it. The LORD smelled the pleasing aroma and said in his heart:
> "Never again will I curse the ground because of humans, even
> though every inclination of the human heart is evil from child-
> hood. And never again will I destroy all living creatures, as I have
> done."   (Genesis 8:20–21)

I want to make a special observation about something that this scene demonstrates: *The last thing God has breathed in is the next thing*

He will exhale. Noah performed the sacrifice, and God "inhaled" the smoky smell, calling it a *"pleasing aroma."* Then God "exhaled" a blessing, a promise. We do the same thing, for better or for worse. We "exhale" the aroma of the atmosphere we have just partaken of. Sometimes that aroma is good, sometimes it's not. But what goes in must come back out. That is why we need to pay attention to our spiritual surroundings.

Our goal should be to share the fragrance of heaven that we have inhaled, as we see in these passages (one each from the Old and New Testaments):

> *Your lips drop sweetness as the honeycomb, my bride; milk and honey are under your tongue. The fragrance of your garments is like the fragrance of Lebanon.* (Song of Songs 4:11)

> *I have all and abound. I am full, having received from Epaphroditus the things sent from you, a sweet-smelling aroma, an acceptable sacrifice, well pleasing to God.* (Philippians 4:18 NKJV)

> OUR GOAL SHOULD BE TO
> SHARE THE FRAGRANCE OF HEAVEN
> THAT WE HAVE INHALED.

THE SCENT OF NEED

One time, I seemed to smell cigarette smoke on a number of the people I was ministering to. It did not make sense to me. I knew for a fact that only a few of them were smokers and that many people could not have not come to my meeting directly from smoke-filled rooms! Baffled, I took the question to prayer, and then I realized what was happening—I was discerning addictions (all kinds of addictions, not necessarily only the addiction to cigarettes). I learned to pose queries to people, inviting them to discuss things so that the truth could come out, followed by repentance, healing, or deliverance. My spiritual sense of smell had become activated and therefore useful for effective prayer.

SENSING GOOD AND EVIL

As you develop your spiritual senses of taste and smell, I want to offer you further help for discerning the difference between good and evil. Consider the following dichotomies:

1. Good exalts God. Evil exalts a person.

2. Good stands the test of time. Evil rushes you to fast conclusions.

3. Good aligns with the Word of God. Evil "paints outside the lines."

4. Good upholds purity. Evil allures you into perversity.

5. Good promotes solid doctrine. Evil promulgates twisted belief systems.

6. Good values community. Evil advocates isolationism.

7. Good values humility. Evil leads to elitism.

Most of these comparisons are self-explanatory, but in number 3, where I say that evil "paints outside the lines," I am referring to the way that misinterpretations of Scripture lead to its misapplication. Human nature is susceptible to the temptation to exaggerate a truth in order to puff up ego—all in the name of healthy, "cutting edge" curiosity and innovation, of course. For example, I know a highly gifted man who persisted in painting outside the lines of sound doctrine. When he explored the ideas of "entertaining angels unawares" (see Hebrews 13:2 KJV) and the *"great cloud of witnesses"* (Hebrews 12:1), he got off track. Instead of staying grounded in the Word and in his church community, he followed his unsanctified curiosity. Now he is off teaching that he can communicate with aliens on other planets.

On a more ordinary level, we can be lured too easily into overstatements. Subconsciously, we may want to impress others, so we embellish our stories. Or we state with certainty something that has been left fairly ambiguous in Scripture. In our striving for personal significance, we may try just about anything to look more spiritual than other people. If someone else says he saw an angel, then the angel *I* saw will be bigger than his, or more impressive than Gabriel, or whatever.

It is far better to avoid any add-ons, and to express your perceptions in measured terms. Stick with honesty by qualifying your statements. For instance, you might say something like, "In my current thinking..." or "I began to sense something..." or "I'm not sure whether this is part of a vision or not...." It is perfectly reasonable to say, "I don't know exactly what this means, but this is what I experienced," and your sharing is no less credible or valuable simply because you do not claim to understand it.

No one in the body of Christ has explored discernment through taste and smell as much as discernment through other means, so it is easier to get misled or mixed up when trying to interpret symbolism in relation to these senses. For example, you might think you smell rotten eggs in the church sanctuary. It must mean something's rotten in the life of the church, right? Well, it is easy to confuse that smell with the smell of ammonia, which is a powerful cleansing agent. What is the proper application? It will depend upon your role in the church and the subsequent guidance of the Holy Spirit. Do not jump to conclusions just because you once heard someone interpret a particular smell in a certain way.

> WHEN EXERCISING DISCERNMENT
> THROUGH TASTE AND SMELL,
> WE NEED TO RELY ON PRAYER,
> THE INTERNAL WITNESS OF
> THE HOLY SPIRIT, THE PRINCIPLES OF
> THE WORD OF GOD, OUR PREVIOUS
> EXPERIENCES, AND THE "FRUIT TEST."

Stay humble, always. You can never understand everything. That is why you keep asking the Holy Spirit questions. That is why you compare notes with people you trust. Test everything. Rely on prayer, the internal witness of the Holy Spirit, the principles of the Word of God, your previous experiences, and the "fruit test": What results from this revelation? Confusion and fear or joy and peace? Freedom or captivity?

Please note that, as with every other spiritual endowment, no one individual possesses the capacity to do everything equally well. Where discernment and sensing are concerned, women are often more attuned than men are, or at least they seem to be sensitive to different things. Do not denigrate the sensitivities of others around you just because you cannot get on the same wavelength. We need each other in the body of Christ. Husbands and wives need each other. Ministry teams need each other. We must walk together in cooperation, not in competition.

REACHING FOR A HIGHER REALM

When you see mature believers whose senses have been more fully activated than yours, absorb as much as you can by observing them in action. Applaud their integrity and sensitivity; do not waste time being jealous of them. I am thinking of a young (to me!) man named Jerame Nelson who lives in California with his wife and family. When I see him ministering prophetically, I can truly believe that my generation's spiritual "ceiling" is serving as the next generation's "floor." As he brings God's truth into refreshingly sharp focus, or smells the sweet fragrance of the presence of the Lord, I can tell that he is someone who knows how to surrender his senses to the Holy Spirit in order to allow them to be heightened. He inspires me! Personally, I want to be aligned with people like that, and to collaborate with them in refining the work of the Lord in our time.

This is especially important because, when it comes to employing our senses of taste and smell or combinations of sense-based leadings, we need all the help we can get. People may have experiences in these areas, but in-depth teaching about them is a different matter. At present, we might not be able to get as much information on this subject as we would like from Christian resources, simply because it has not been a major topic among Christian teachers. This will change, though, over a process of time as more leaders experience receiving revelation through their senses and combine their experiences and biblical knowledge to develop helpful instruction. In the meantime, I encourage you to seek out like-minded believers who are open to the various ways in which God wants to speak to us, and to gain more experience in discerning revelation, remembering to ask the Lord to confirm the revelation and to give you wisdom for its application.

The gifts of the Spirit are like a rainbow. One color ends and another color begins without a clear demarcation. So also with discernment—we apprehend spiritual information in a variety of overlapping ways, and it comes through more than one of our senses. Only through dedicated practice can we learn to ride with the Spirit of God with fluid movements across the supernatural realm.

PRAYER OF A DISCERNING HEART

Holy Spirit, finger of God, I ask You to touch me today. Lord, make Your written Word come alive to me. Illumine it and make it into a *rhema*, a spoken and revelatory word. Make *me* come alive, too. Enhance and heighten my senses—especially where some of them may have become dull—through the gifts of Your Spirit, Your anointing, and Your grace. I want to receive and discern Your revelation in my life. I want to encounter You even if it takes me beyond my intellectual limits and comfort zone.

Help me to discern not only what You are communicating to me, but also the activities of other spiritual and natural forces, to whatever degree will prove useful to Your purposes. Help me to know when and how to share the revelations You give me.

I present myself to You. I lack understanding; help me to trust Your understanding even in the midst of trying circumstances. I lean into Your love. Cause me to cling closely to You all the time. In Jesus's precious name, amen.

6

KNOWING: THE SIXTH SENSE

"'Who has known the mind of the LORD that he may instruct
Him?' But we have the mind of Christ."
—1 Corinthians 2:16 (NKJV)

I was up on a cliff overlooking the angry February Adriatic Sea, getting ready to preach in a community center in the city of Shëngjin, Albania, where the gospel had not been preached in living memory. There were no church buildings for our meeting; this was in 1992, soon after the fall of Communism there. I had no idea what to say to these oppressed people, so I had gone outside to pray. "Lord, what do You have for these people of ancient Albania?" I asked.

A name floated across my mind: "Sarah."

Huh? But what word do You have for these people tonight?

"Sarah." *That's it?* I didn't feel anything special. I didn't get any explanation. The name occurred to me a third time: "Sarah," just a woman's name. I knew that *Sarah* was not even an Albanian name, and I did not think it had to do with Abraham's wife Sarah. So I pushed the thought aside and went back to my hotel room to get ready for the evening meeting.

That night, I had to start preaching sooner than I expected because there was no music, no worship. It did not seem like a very good beginning. Through my interpreter, I told the hundred and twenty or so people (all of whom were wearing their winter coats inside because we were in an unheated building) something about myself, and I mentioned the idea that God sets us free.

We were not connecting. Then I had a "knowing." I remembered the name "Sarah," and I turned to my translator and said, "How do you say the name 'Sarah' in the Albanian language?"

"Sabrina," he replied.

"Is anyone here named Sabrina?" I asked the group. Three-fourths of the way back, a woman raised her hand.

I did not know what to do next, so I said, "Sabrina, please step out into the aisle." She did so, and I saw that she was wearing a thick winter coat. I was hoping that when she stepped out, I would get more from the Holy Spirit. I didn't. So I moved her closer: "Sabrina, please come up here to the front."

I still did not know what else to say, so I told my interpreter, "Say this: 'Your name is Sabrina.'" (Although we already had that one down.) Then I added, "You've never in your life heard the gospel of Jesus Christ preached." I did not need divine revelation for that information. Nobody in the entire city had ever heard the gospel before. I was just priming the pump.

Then other knowings started coming: "And you're thirty-two years old." *Oh, God. I hope this is right.* She shook her head in assent. I added, "And you have a tumor in your left breast, and Jesus wants to heal you." There was quite a stir in the crowd. Apparently this was somewhat common knowledge to the people in the room.

The fear of the Lord came over the place—awe and wonder. Sabrina was startled, to say the least, and she got saved on the spot. So did others. Every one of those lovely people experienced a "God encounter." For me, this was a taste of breaking open a new territory for the gospel of Jesus Christ in true apostolic fashion!

Eventually, everyone went home for the night, but that is not the end of the story. Three of us needed to get to the next city where we were lodging. We attempted to hail a taxicab, although it was a dark and rainy night and cars were scarce in Albania. A car pulled over. It crossed my mind that this was like when Philip got into that chariot in the book of Acts. (See Acts 8:26–40.) I got into the front seat and started to tell the driver about the exciting things that had just happened in the community center.

Suddenly, he began to tremble—because Sabrina was his wife! He was a Muslim, and he had never heard the gospel before, either. By the time we reached our destination, he had gotten saved, too. I sometimes wonder what it was like later that night when he returned home to his wife.

JUST KNOWING

I like to use the above illustration because it is an excellent example of how the sense of knowing works. The name "Sarah" had just sort of floated to the surface of my mind, as had the other "knowings" that night. I did not hear, see, taste, touch, or smell anything. I just knew. Knowing is like a sixth sense.

This method of receiving revelation may seem out of the ordinary to us, but we should not be surprised when things work this way. After all, as you just read in the Scripture at the beginning of this chapter, "*we have the mind of Christ.*" Everyone who is a believer has the mind of Christ. That means you as well as me. That meant me when I was standing by the Adriatic Sea in 1992, and it means you sitting in your chair reading these words right now. To be sure, this does not mean that you or I have the mind of Christ in its entirety, which would be impossible. But taken together, as members of the body of Christ, we can begin to think His thoughts. I have one aspect of the mind of Christ and you have another aspect. We depend upon each other.

A couple of decades ago, this supernatural knowing used to be referred to as "receiving impressions." I remember being told, "Give expression to the impression," and I find that terminology useful to this day, since impressions are fleeting glimpses, and that is how this kind of knowing comes to your attention; impressions sort of flash across the screen of your mind. And if you somehow fail to capture an impression, it will soon fade into oblivion.

It may be in the form of a premonition or guidance: *I'm in the right place at the right time.* It may be like a sense of déjà vu: *Hey, I've seen this before! I've heard this before. I've experienced this before. I think I actually know something about this.*

Suddenly you know—and you know that you know—and you know that God put it into your mind. It creates a kind of God-confidence that you did not realize you lacked.

It is too easy to ignore these things. As with the impression "Sarah," knowings do not always seem to make sense. And they can occur when you least expect them. You must become intentional about remembering them, much as you become intentional about remembering your dreams when you wake up. You will never encounter a large angel telling you, "Remember this!" (At least I never have.) In your life, you need to create an openness to receiving revelation, as well as to develop a disposition for retaining it.

> CREATE AN OPENNESS TO
> RECEIVING REVELATION,
> AND DEVELOP A DISPOSITION
> FOR RETAINING IT.

A "KNOWING"—OR A RANDOM THOUGHT?

How can you distinguish between a spiritual knowing sent by God and a random thought generated by your overactive imagination? I would recommend asking God for confirmation. The confirmation might take various forms, for example a repeated mention of the same words. God always seems to confirm words by the testimony of two or three witnesses, and He confirms His ideas throughout the Bible.

(See, for example, Deuteronomy 19:15; John 8:13–18; 2 Corinthians 13:1.)

What if you try to remember the knowing, but you forget it anyway? I would say, "Relax and trust." Do not lean on your own understanding. Trust that if you did receive a genuine knowing of some sort, God will bring it back to your mind at the right time. God's word never returns to Him empty, as Isaiah wrote:

> "For My thoughts are not your thoughts, nor are your ways My ways," declares the LORD. "For as the heavens are higher than the earth, so are My ways higher than your ways and My thoughts than your thoughts. For as the rain and the snow come down from heaven, and do not return there without watering the earth and making it bear and sprout, and furnishing seed to the sower and bread to the eater; so will My word be which goes forth from My mouth; it will not return to Me empty, without accomplishing what I desire, and without succeeding in the matter for which I sent it."
>
> (Isaiah 55:8–11 NASB)

God, who planted the thought in your mind, will bring the revelation to fruition. "For I am confident of this very thing, that He who began a good work in you will perfect it until the day of Christ Jesus" (Philippians 1:6 NASB). Along the way, He may also decide to reveal to you hindrances that are making it difficult for you to retain what He shows you.

Remember, a knowing is just a flash, a small thought from the mind of an infinite God; it is not a whole paragraph or a thesis or a book. Once you remember the key word or concept, a few more details may come into focus, but you are not responsible for more than your small share of God's knowledge.

YOU CAN HAVE THE MIND OF CHRIST

Even before Jesus appeared in the flesh, God manifested His knowledge and wisdom through certain individuals. For example, remember the sons of Issachar:

Of the sons of Issachar, men who understood the times, with knowledge of what Israel should do, their chiefs were two hundred; and all their kinsmen were at their command.

(1 Chronicles 12:32 NASB)

It is of paramount importance for the church to find people today who understand the times and who know what leaders should do. Lots of prophetic people get discernment about the times and seasons, but only a few of them know what to do with that information. This is the kind of knowing that we call "wisdom."

By observing Jesus's life in the Scriptures, we can see more clearly what the mind of Christ looks like, and what we can aim for. In the Gospels, we read, *"Jesus knowing their thoughts said, 'Why are you think-ing evil in your hearts?'"* (Matthew 9:4 NASB). He just knew what people were thinking. *"Jesus, knowing what they were thinking in their heart, took a child and stood him by His side..."* (Luke 9:47 NASB). He knew what the Father was thinking, too: *"Jesus, knowing that the Father had given all things into His hands, and that He had come forth from God and was going back to God..."* (John 13:3 NASB).

We must get to the place in our lives where minor (or even major) disappointments or disruptions do not throw us off course, because we have the mind of Christ. We need to be so close to Him that we can ask for guidance or peace or grace or wisdom. That is the lifestyle of a disciple that we see portrayed in the New Testament. Consider the following Scriptures; just read them all together:

If any of you lacks wisdom, you should ask God, who gives gener-ously to all without finding fault, and it will be given to you. But when you ask, you must believe and not doubt, because the one who doubts is like a wave of the sea, blown and tossed by the wind. That person should not expect to receive anything from the Lord. Such a person is double-minded and unstable in all they do.

(James 1:5–8)

You do not have because you do not ask God. (James 4:2)

Of Him you are in Christ Jesus, who became for us wisdom from God—and righteousness and sanctification and redemption—that, as it is written, "He who glories, let him glory in the LORD."
(1 Corinthians 1:30–31 NKJV)

For "who has known the mind of the LORD that he may instruct Him?" But we have the mind of Christ.
(1 Corinthians 2:16 NKJV)

Therefore I tell you, whatever you ask for in prayer, believe that you have received it, and it will be yours. (Mark 11:24)

> IT IS PARAMOUNT FOR
> THE CHURCH TODAY TO
> FIND PEOPLE WHO UNDERSTAND
> THE TIMES AND WHO KNOW
> WHAT LEADERS SHOULD DO.

When you ask God for His help, personalize it: "Lord, I lack _____. You have a vast supply, and it has been made available to me through Christ Jesus." Be specific. Rest in the assurance that He has heard you. Wait patiently and believingly with openness and receptivity.

We receive in different ways at different times. An impression might float up into your heart and become illuminated on the screen of your mind. Or, a passage of Scripture might capture your attention and spur you into action. You pray, *Oh, okay Lord. You want me to study to show myself approved?*[17] *Do you mean I should get some training in* _____? And He responds, "Uh-huh." (That sense of concurrence and approval is a knowing, too.)

---

17. See 2 Timothy 2:15.

The process is supernatural, and it is a little elusive, but it is not overly mystical or weird. It is just your life with the Spirit of Christ. And with practice, it can become supernaturally natural. You, too, can be a discerner of good and evil.

KNOWINGS AND THE GIFTS OF THE SPIRIT

In my book *Releasing Spiritual Gifts Today*, I highlighted the gifts of the Holy Spirit, which include the nine most important ones: discerning of spirits, word of wisdom, word of knowledge, faith, gifts of healings, kinds of tongues, interpretation of tongues, prophecy, and workings of miracles. (See 1 Corinthians 12:8–10.) The sixth sense of knowing can come into play in support of any of the gifts, most obviously with the gift of the word of knowledge.

A word of knowledge answers questions for other people that you may not even know about. A word of knowledge is not going to be about you (because you know your own questions already, and many of the answers). Such words can be remarkably specific, supplying names, dates, locations, and other convincing details that only God could know. They come through seeing, hearing, and other types of sensing—and through your thoughts, through knowing.

For example, once I was ministering to people in a back room of the Anaheim Vineyard church when a man walked in for his ministry appointment. He was not wearing a name tag, and we had not been given any information about him prior to this, but I saw the name "Steve" written above his head in the air. Then I just knew—I do not know how I knew, but I did—that Steve was not his name. Sometimes when this happens, you can gently probe the person for information, asking something like, "Does the name 'Steve' mean anything to you?" But this time, I felt fairly sure that I should cast about in the Spirit for the answer. Internally, I started asking what, when, and how questions to the Holy Spirit. I wondered if any passage from the Word might help clarify things. I considered possible issues he might be dealing with. Then, just like that, another knowing floated up: *Oh. Steve is his spiritual overseer.* Along with that came a suggestion of a question: *How long does he have to stay under Steve?*

So I engaged the man in conversation. "I see the name 'Steve' written over your head, but your name is not Steve. Is that correct?"

"Yes."

"I know that you're from the state of Ohio and that you have come in with a question. Steve is your overseer, your leader, and you want to move on to something else. You are wondering, 'How long do I have to stay under Steve?'"

His eyes got big. He told me that just before he had walked into the room, he had stated those exact words to his friend: "How long do I have to stay under Steve?"

Then I looked at him and gave him the answer: "You've got to give it one more year, and then you're going to know; then you will be released to go out on your own." I added that I felt that someone else would give him his own ministry, but the time had not come quite yet. In the meantime, he was to serve faithfully under Steve.

That sort of knowledge does not come forth frequently. But a somewhat dramatic testimony such as this one helps to illustrate what the gift of the word of knowledge looks like, coupled with the senses of knowing, feeling, and seeing.

Similarly, the operation of other gifts can be enhanced by the sense of knowing. In the story about Sabrina, I would say that the gift of prophecy was used to bring encouraging words that built up the people who heard them.

The gift of faith is often received via knowings as well. The gift of faith is like having a portion of God's faith, a supernatural surge of confidence in God. Oral Roberts used to say, "I know that I know that I know that I know." Knowings give you a deep-down gut feeling that you just cannot shake off. You might not have words for it. You do not hear or see or smell anything. You just know. In a similar way, knowings can help you use the gift of discerning of spirits. You can perceive the motivation of the spirit behind whatever manifestation you are observing with your other senses.

WALKING IN DIVINE INTELLIGENCE

I did a webinar with Patricia King about accessing divine intelligence—insights, revelations, solutions, and strategies from God. We posted it on our respective teaching websites.[18] A lot of what I share in the webinar comes from studying the life of Daniel.

As we read in the first chapter of the book of Daniel, referring to the young man Daniel and his companions, *"As for these four youths, God gave them knowledge and intelligence in every branch of literature and wisdom; Daniel even understood all kinds of visions and dreams"* (Daniel 1:17 NASB). They did not receive this knowledge and intelligence because they had earned it; neither had they studied to obtain it. They did study in the leadership training program set up by the king of Babylon, but their exceptional level of knowledge and intelligence was a pure gift from God. And it was not just Daniel—who ended up being the best-known of the four men—who received it. God gave it to each one of them. Their knowledge and intelligence made it possible for the four exiles from Judah to flourish in the court of Nebuchadnezzar.

Daniel understood where his abilities came from. An angel who later conveyed prophecy to Daniel affirmed, *"The people who know their God will display strength and take action"* (Daniel 11:32 NASB). At that time, Daniel was given a glimpse into the future and was told that knowledge would only increase after he was gone: *"But you, Daniel, shut up the words, and seal the book until the time of the end; many shall run to and fro, and knowledge shall increase"* (Daniel 12:4 NKJV).

I used to think that verse referred to only one category of knowledge. I thought it meant how people would eventually have the Gutenberg printing press and encyclopedias and the Internet. Of course, to some extent that is what it means. But it could also have to do with what Isaiah called the *"spirit of knowledge"* when he wrote about seven "spirits," or attributes, of God, of which He gives portions

---

18. See www.XPMedia.com and www.GodEncounters.com.

to His people as gifts and graces: the Spirit of the Lord, the spirit of wisdom, the spirit of understanding, the spirit of counsel, the spirit of strength or might, the spirit of knowledge, and the spirit of the fear of the Lord. (See Isaiah 11:1–3 NASB.) Regarding the spirit of knowledge—posing the question undogmatically—could it be that not only will knowledge become more available to more people as time goes on, but also that revelatory knowledge will increase, especially as the latter days grow shorter?

This kind of knowledge does not simply fill our minds with more information. Rather, it gives us faith and hope: "*Since we belong to the day, let us be sober, putting on faith and love as a breastplate, and the hope of salvation as a helmet*" (1 Thessalonians 5:8). As the positive expectation of good, hope has to do with our minds, our thoughts. Hope holds solutions to our questions. Knowings and divine intelligence make it possible for us to live in hope and to give hope away.

We need to be ambassadors of hope, bringing hope solutions to the world as the last days continue to unfold. As I put it in my book *Finding Hope*: "The world needs vibrant believers who have won their way through monumental obstacles and who can show the way of hope. Hope ambassadors know hope inside out. They breathe hope, live hope, exhibit hope, and light up their sphere of influence with hope."[19]

I want to be one who discerns times and seasons, who walks in divine intelligence, and who offers hope solutions. I believe God is inviting you to come along with me on the journey. I want to be a son of Issachar in my generation, and to help raise up more sons and daughters in the faith.

> KNOWINGS AND DIVINE INTELLIGENCE
> MAKE IT POSSIBLE FOR US TO
> LIVE IN HOPE AND TO GIVE HOPE AWAY.

19. James W. Goll, *Finding Hope* (Racine, WI: BroadStreet Publishing Group, 2015), 154.

REACHING FOR A HIGHER REALM

As we begin to hear God's voice more clearly through our senses, there is the risk that we may slip into pride, which will immediately start to shut down the flow from heaven. If that happens, we find that we must manufacture feelings and thoughts that used to bubble up from the Holy Spirit. We tend to turn off the spiritual checks and balances and rely on ourselves.

The cure is simple: humility. Acknowledge that you are special to God only because He created you and He loves you unconditionally, not because of your incredible giftedness and amazing insights.

Always remember the main and plain truth: God is good. All the time. He does not browbeat people. He does not stand over you like a taskmaster. When difficulties assail you, it is not because He is unleashing punishment on you. He always wants to show you a clear path.

Also, do not forget about the importance of having rest and peace. You can't serve God at a frantic pace for very long, and your internal noise will drown out His quiet voice. Knowings will float to the surface only if you are not splashing around, afraid of drowning due to your circumstances. God is much bigger than any issue you may ever face, and He is not worried at all. He does not have sweaty palms; He is not wringing His hands in heaven, fretting over the lack of solutions. Again, heaven's revelation brings hope solutions to earth's problems.

God does not expect every person to have a platform ministry or some kind of extensive prayer ministry. Even those who do have a public ministry do not live every moment on a pinnacle. You might be a mom with six kids. You might be a single dad. You do not have the time or funds to go to faraway meetings and conferences. That is OK. God loves it when you are washing dishes. He loves it when you are baking pies. He loves it when you are driving to work. He loves it when you sit in your chair and think you are doing nothing, but you are being content, and you have quieted your soul. *"The kingdom of God is...righteousness, peace and joy in the Holy Spirit"* (Romans 14:17).

"And the peace of God, which transcends all understanding, will guard your hearts and your minds in Christ Jesus" (Philippians 4:7).

Always remember, we serve a good, good God, and He has good gifts to help His kids grow in discernment wherever they find themselves. He wants you to grow in receiving and discerning revelation. It is part of your inheritance, your birthright!

PRAYER OF A DISCERNING HEART

Heavenly Father, in Jesus's name, I present my mind to You. I have learned from Your Word that I do not have because I do not ask You. Therefore, I am quick to admit my need and to declare Your sure supply. I ask for Your divine thoughts and wisdom to be released in my mind. I ask for an increase of Your peace that passes understanding—so that I can relax into a new level of knowing what You want to show me.

I surrender my physical and spiritual mind to the Holy Spirit, and I put on the helmet of hope. I want to effervesce with the life of God. Thank You for giving me a sixth sense, an ability to know that rises above my own capability. By the grace of God, I believe that I am receiving an increase of Your revelation in my heart and mind. For Jesus Christ's sake, amen.

SECTION TWO:
DISCERNING REVELATION

Not all revelation comes from God, and not even all of what appears to be spiritual comes from the Holy Spirit. This is why we need to learn not only how to receive revelation, but also how to discern the essential differences between the voice of God, the voice of Satan, and the voices of our own minds. In the following six chapters, you will learn to distinguish what you are sensing so that you will not be deceived.

Chapter 7 is on "testing the spirits." The unseen supernatural reality around us is populated with both angels and demons, and human beings are notoriously poor at telling the difference between good spirits and bad ones. In this chapter, I reinforce crucial foundational points such as how to become a God-centered person and the importance of honoring the authority that God has put in your life for your protection. I also offer nine key scriptural tests for revelation.

Chapter 8 helps you to elude spiritual deception. "To be forewarned is to be forearmed," and I arm you for the battle by telling you what to watch out for. I explain how you can know the identity of evil spirits and how to allow God's light to expose the enemy.

Chapter 9, about exposing demonic influences, concerns the practical process of discerning these effects and delivering people from the enemy. I have concentrated my attention on the most common—and often the most subtle—demonic influences, including the religious spirit, the political spirit, the spirit of fear and intimidation, and the antichrist spirit.

Chapter 10 shows you how avoid Satan's traps. For example, most of us have wrestled with the issue of pretense, masquerading as someone else in order to get the approval of others. Though this seems to bring rewards, pretense is clearly a trap that will prevent spiritual perceptivity. Other Satanic traps must also be exposed in order to be avoided, such as false authority and the spirit of offense.

Chapter 11 describes how the church's culture of wisdom and faith can make it a safe place for all. The victory that overcomes the world is our faith, but our faith is often tested. We need safe places to resort to, where the faith and discernment of others can shore ours up. By living out the core truths that we preach, we can create such a culture of faith in our churches.

The final chapter lifts up the most glorious revelation of all—the incarnation. By enabling us to receive His revelation and to discern His messages out of the chaos of many competing voices, Jesus empowers us to become a revelation of His presence in the world. Incarnational Christianity is the strongest witness of all in this dark world. By receiving and discerning revelation from God, we shine the light of God into the darkness.

7

TESTING THE SPIRITS: "DO NOT BELIEVE EVERY SPIRIT"

"Dear friends, do not believe every spirit, but test the spirits to see whether they are from God, because many false prophets have gone out into the world."
—1 John 4:1

The first six chapters of this book have been about surrendering your senses to the Holy Spirit to better receive revelation, and they have touched on the idea of verifying the trustworthiness of what you may receive, but now we need to dive in headfirst. We must take a detailed look at how you learn to decide—sometimes instantaneously—what to do with the various forms of revelation you receive. Remember, it is by practice that you learn to discern good and evil, and such discernment is of critical importance in the days in which we live.

DON'T BE NAÏVE!

Not all revelation comes from God, and not even all of what appears to be spiritual comes from the Holy Spirit. As the theme Scripture for this chapter makes clear, it is imperative to learn how to *"test the spirits"* in order to determine if they are serving God or the enemy. Do not be naïve! The unseen supernatural reality around us is populated with both angels and demons, and human beings are notoriously poor at telling the difference between good spirits and bad ones.

Only naïve people will believe everything that comes across their screen. Satan is always lurking just out of sight, plotting wickedness against God's people, and we must not be ignorant of his schemes. (See 1 Peter 5:8; 2 Corinthians 2:11.) He especially loves to deceive the very people who are trying to learn how to receive revelation from God. Let's stay ahead of that, OK?

Realize that you can't elude the enemy just by pretending he is not there. He is. You will find him around every corner. During your lifetime, you will be exposed to plenty of evil, and you might even need to learn about some of it. But you do not have to fall for it. To stay clear, you need to discover how to discern the difference between the devil's doings, God's workings, and everything in between.

I have run across some people who hold back from testing the spirits, saying, "Well, I don't want to offend the Holy Spirit." Huh? I guess they think it would bother God if they acted suspicious about something that may or may not originate from Him. That kind of reasoning does not hold water. Just look at Scripture. False prophets are real, and God wants you to spurn them. He wants you to be alert and to test the spirits. He wants to help you do this, and your mistakes do not worry Him. He is pleased when you make the right distinctions and lean into Him for guidance and wisdom.

Other people may read the above Scripture about testing the spirits and get a little nervous about dealing with evil powers. "Test every spirit? No way do I want to risk my welfare by calling out Satan's demons. Please don't make me do that!" To them, I can only quote the words that Paul wrote to "Timid Timothy": "*God has not given us a spirit of fear, but of power and of love and of a sound mind*" (2 Timothy 1:7 NKJV). We have not received a spirit of intimidation or bondage, but a spirit of courage, effectiveness, and love. Trust the Holy Spirit to take care of you when you confront evil. Put your trust in the God who can protect you and who will deliver whoever calls on His name. (See Joel 2:32.)

It is not that every mistaken word comes straight from the devil's mouth. Some of it is more like junk mail—not of much value, but not especially harmful, either. Again, you need discernment to determine whether a word is from God, from Satan, or a mixture from a human mind. Remember—you do not need to discern and test the spirits solo; you always have the Holy Spirit helping you. Relax and let Him show you what to do.

> WE HAVE NOT RECEIVED A SPIRIT OF
> INTIMIDATION OR BONDAGE,
> BUT A SPIRIT OF
> COURAGE, EFFECTIVENESS, AND LOVE.

DISCERNMENT BASICS

Some key foundational points are in order before we move on to the details. Most basic of all: *Be a God-centered person.* Be a God-chaser more than you are a demon-buster. Even if you have a deliverance ministry, you should not be demon-centered but rather God-centered.

As a God-centered person, worship your heart out. Not only should it be your natural response to His greatness, but you can expect to be cleansed and filled anew with His Spirit when you worship. When you worship His majesty, His Majesty will visit you! Praise Him. Pour out your heart to Him. Bow to Him. Dance before Him. Enjoy His presence. Then it will be a much simpler matter to both recognize Him and discern something that is foreign to Him.

Another basic discernment key has to do with the authority figures in your life. Christians who blindly follow their leaders in the name of proper submission are prone to deception. Ask yourself, "Have I given away to others the power of making my own decisions?" If you have, you have already removed yourself from taking direction from God Himself, and you are likely to find yourself in trouble at some point.

Trustworthy leaders point you to God, not to themselves. Responsible authority figures never need to make you feel that they are indispensable to your well-being.

Now, it is true that Scripture tells us to submit to those in authority over us. (See, for example, Romans 13:1–2; Hebrews 13:17; 1 Peter 2:13–14.) How can you reconcile that instruction with what I just said? We can get a better idea of what proper submission to authority looks like if we note the way trustworthy people in the Bible modeled it. Daniel, for example, submitted to everything that was expected of him as an exile in the court of the king of Babylon—unless it transgressed God's clear command. So he would not bow down to a false god, even under the threat of losing his life. But he would submit to almost everything else demanded of him. And when he objected to a royal command, he did so with respect. (See, for example, Daniel 1:6–16.)

Jesus knew that the Roman taxation system was unjust, but He still paid His taxes. (See Matthew 17:24–27.) Additionally, Peter and John showed respect to the authorities and obeyed them, except when doing so would put them in disobedience to God, as we see in their response to the Sanhedrin:

> *Then they called them in again and commanded them not to speak or teach at all in the name of Jesus. But Peter and John replied, "Which is right in God's eyes: to listen to you, or to him? You be the judges! As for us, we cannot help speaking about what we have seen and heard."* (Acts 4:18–20)

Daniel, Jesus, Peter, and John honored those who were in human authority over them, but they honored God first and foremost. You can always honor, but you do not always have to obey. For instance, if you have submitted yourself voluntarily to an authority figure such as a pastor, you are free to leave if you wish, being decisive but respectful.

If you find it difficult to honor a particularly unworthy authority figure, I recommend praying for that person. Paul wrote, "*I urge that entreaties and prayers, petitions and thanksgivings, be made on behalf of all men, for kings and all who are in authority*" (1 Timothy 2:1–2 NASB). We know that most of the political and religious leaders in Paul's time were *dis*honorable men, and yet Paul recommended honoring them by praying for them. Such prayers have the added benefit of changing our hearts, too.

DISCERNMENT POWER POINTS

As you learn the ropes of testing the spirits, remember this: *there is power in speaking God's Word*. Just try it. Read Scripture out loud. Repeat one of God's promises. You will see how darkness gets exposed by the light. The more you do it, from your heart, the more authority you will discover behind this spiritual discipline. We must remember that we are part of a speech-activated kingdom!

In addition, *there is power in forgiveness*. When we fail to forgive our brother from the heart, according to the teachings of Jesus, we actually get turned over to "the tormenters." (See Matthew 18:23–35 KJV.) In other words, we get tormented by evil spirits and wicked thoughts. Forgiveness must work both ways—vertically and horizontally—at the same time. Whether we are receiving or giving forgiveness, we are clearing the way for the King to come in glory. Besides freedom from the harassment of evil spirits, clearer discernment is a wonderful by-product of forgiveness.

Most important of all, *there is power in the cross, in the name and blood of Jesus*. This goes alongside the reminder about worship that I mentioned above. When you worship Jesus and extol His name, you end up praising Him for the power of His shed blood. This truth was seared into my heart back during the Jesus People movement when I heard Derek Prince say, "The way of the cross leads home." So simple. So complete.

When Jesus was dying on the cross and said, *"It is finished"* (John 19:30), He meant that He was about to expire, but also that His purpose for coming to earth as a Man and suffering so greatly had been accomplished. He had done the impossible; He had bridged the gap between sin-saturated humanity and the purity of heaven. He had defeated Satan, sickness, and death. Everything every one of us could ever need, He obtained at the cross. He was the only one who could have done what He did. His work was perfect and complete, and through Him we can defeat all the power of the enemy. (See Luke 10:19.) "The Cross"—that says it all.

> THERE IS POWER IN SPEAKING GOD'S WORD, IN FORGIVENESS, AND IN THE CROSS—IN THE NAME AND BLOOD OF JESUS.

TESTING THE SPIRITS—BIBLICAL AND NECESSARY

In one Scripture after another, we are urged to test the spirits. Here are a couple of good examples:

Do not despise prophecies. Test all things; hold fast what is good.
(1 Thessalonians 5:20–21 NKJV)

Dear friends, do not believe every spirit, but test the spirits to see whether they are from God, because many false prophets have gone out into the world. This is how you can recognize the Spirit of God: Every spirit that acknowledges that Jesus Christ has come in the flesh is from God, but every spirit that does not acknowledge Jesus is not from God. This is the spirit of the antichrist, which you have heard is coming and even now is already in the world.
(1 John 4:1–3)

From these passages, you can learn some very practical tips for flushing out the Evil One, and you can begin to see how the testing of spirits becomes a regular feature of your lifestyle. One part of exercising discernment is learning the moment-by-moment assessment process. Alert to the possibilities, you scan your surroundings before you commit yourself to a course of action.

The other part of exercising discernment requires patient observation: you must observe the kind of fruit that grows over time.[20] Gifts are bestowed on a specific occasion, but fruit needs time to develop. Other tests may yield immediate results, but the "fruit test" takes a little longer. You cannot determine the quality of fruit until it has grown and matured. Thus, you have the initial test and you also have the moment later on when you test the fruit.

NINE SCRIPTURAL TESTS OF REVELATION

The following tests of revelation, based on the authority of God's Word, always work. I have taught them in many different cities, nations, and cultures, and their truths are universal. I am going to assign them numbers to help you remember and apply them. Each revelation, large or small, can be tested against these scriptural statements:

1. *The revelation must build up the recipient.* The end result of all revelation from God is to build up, admonish, and encourage the people of God. Anything else is suspect. Paul sums it up best:

> But the one who prophesies speaks to people for their strengthening, encouraging and comfort.... What then shall we say, brothers and sisters? When you come together, each of you has a hymn, or a word of instruction, a revelation, a tongue or an interpretation. Everything must be done so that the church may be built up.
> (1 Corinthians 14:3, 26)

Note that sometimes a word can start out sounding negative, but if we are patient, we will be rewarded with restored hope and a promise. (See for example Jeremiah 1:5, 10.)

2. *The revelation must honor the recorded Word of God.* All true revelation agrees with both the letter and the spirit of Scripture. When the Holy Spirit says "yes and amen" in a revelation (see 2 Corinthians 1:20), He has already said the same in Scripture. The Spirit of God never contradicts Himself. One of the most subtle demonic attacks

---

20. *"Make a tree good and its fruit will be good, or make a tree bad and its fruit will be bad, for a tree is recognized by its fruit"* (Matthew 12:33).

against the authority of the Word of God is the widespread idea that "there is no such thing as absolute authority" (some might say that "all authority is relative"). Be aware of a wishy-washy, liberal approach to theology and the authority of the Scriptures, because...

> *All Scripture is God-breathed and is useful for teaching, rebuking, correcting and training in righteousness, so that the servant of God may be thoroughly equipped for every good work.*
> (2 Timothy 3:16–17)

> *As surely as God is faithful, our message to you is not "Yes" and "No." For the Son of God, Jesus Christ, who was preached among you by us...was not "Yes" and "No," but in him it has always been "Yes." For no matter how many promises God has made, they are "Yes" in Christ. And so through him the "Amen" is spoken by us to the glory of God.* (2 Corinthians 1:18–20)

3. *The revelation must glorify God the Father and God the Son.* Jesus said, "[The Holy Spirit] *will glorify me because it is from me that he will receive what he will make known to you*" (John 16:14). And we read in Revelation, "*For the testimony of Jesus is the spirit of prophecy*" (Revelation 19:10 NASB).

4. *The revelation will be established by its fruit.* Here is another reference to keeping an eye on the fruit of a revelation:

> *Watch out for false prophets. They come to you in sheep's clothing, but inwardly they are ferocious wolves. By their fruit you will recognize them. Do people pick grapes from thornbushes, or figs from thistles?* (Matthew 7:15–16)

Is the fruit good or bad? Good fruit will line up with the list in Galatians 5:22–23 that we discussed earlier, "*for the fruit of the Spirit is in all goodness, righteousness, and truth*" (Ephesians 5:9 NKJV). But if the fruit lines up with the preceding verses in Galatians (see Galatians 5:19–21), you know the "revelation" is going to be bad news. If something calls you into these realms, do not follow: pride, boastfulness, exaggeration, dishonesty, covetousness, financial irresponsibility, licentiousness, all forms of immorality, such as adultery and fornication, addictions, and even a party spirit. These fruits are rotten and will poison people's lives. You can be sure that any supposed revelation that results in such rotten fruit has flowed from a source other than the Holy Spirit.

5. *Predictive revelations will be fulfilled.* This is a straightforward test, although it might take quite some time to verify:

> *You may say to yourselves, "How can we know when a message has not been spoken by the LORD?" If what a prophet proclaims in the name of the LORD does not take place or come true, that is a message the Lord has not spoken. That prophet has spoken presumptuously, so do not be alarmed.*   (Deuteronomy 18:21–22)

If a revelation contains a prediction concerning the future and it does not come true, you can discount it as not coming from God. There are a few possible exceptions to this guideline: (1) God has given humankind a free will to choose His ways—or not; (2) some authentic words carry critical consequences unless people repent—and the repentance occurs;[21] or (3) the fulfillment of a word can occur a long time afterward.[22]

6. *The revelation must direct people to Jesus.* Even if a prophet is highly gifted and can produce miracles, do not believe a word they say unless their revelations direct people to Jesus. Jesus warned against false prophets who produce false signs and wonders:

> *Watch out for false prophets. They come to you in sheep's clothing, but inwardly they are ferocious wolves.... Many false prophets will appear and deceive many people.... For false messiahs and false prophets will appear and perform great signs and wonders to deceive, if possible, even the elect.*   (Matthew 7:15; 24:11, 24)[23]

7. *The revelation must release the spirit of adoption.* What is "*the spirit of adoption*"? It is the assurance of being sons and daughters of God, as

---

21. The city of Nineveh is an example. See the book of Jonah.
22. For example, messianic prophecies.
23. See also Deuteronomy 13:1–5.

opposed to being captive slaves: "*For you have not received a spirit of slavery leading to fear again, but you have received a spirit of adoption as sons by which we cry out, 'Abba! Father!'*" (Romans 8:15 NASB). Slaves experience fear, shame, blame, and unwelcome control. Sons and daughters feel secure; they know they can call out to their Abba for any kind of help at any time.

8. *The revelation must produce life.* Along with the proof of the spirit of adoption, does a revelation produce life—or death—in those who hear it? The rigid "letter of the law" does not produce the new covenant life of the Spirit, as noted by Paul: "*He has made us competent as ministers of a new covenant—not of the letter but of the Spirit; for the letter kills, but the Spirit gives life*" (2 Corinthians 3:6).

> ASK YOURSELF, "DOES THE REVELATION PRODUCE LIFE—OR DEATH— IN THOSE WHO HEAR IT?"

9. *True revelation will be attested to by the Holy Spirit.* This ninth test is the most subjective of them all and must be used in conjunction with the previous tests in order to determine whether or not the Holy Spirit attests to a word as coming from God. "*As his anointing teaches you about all things and as that anointing is real, not counterfeit—just as it has taught you, remain in him*" (1 John 2:27).

We must value the anointing of the Holy Spirit, because He helps us apply every test. We cannot take the anointing of the Spirit for granted, even if we have years and years of experience of walking with God. Besides the general anointing we receive when the Holy Spirit comes to live within us, by which Jesus said we are guided into all truth (see John 16:13), your specific anointing might be for pastoring and mine might be for teaching. But each of us needs to walk within the sphere of grace we have received and value the anointings that have been given to the other members of the body of Christ. We need to rely on each other in the discernment process. Do not compare yourself to others unless seeing their anointing makes you hungry for more of God.

TESTING THE SPIRITS IN ACTION

One time I was ministering with Mahesh Chavda in Eastern Europe, right after Communism was lifted. Everybody in attendance at the meetings was either an unbeliever or a new believer. After Mahesh had preached and given an altar call, he moved down a prayer line, praying briefly for each person in turn. I followed him, praying for people further as I felt led.

Mahesh prayed for one young man, and he "fell out," overwhelmed by the power of the Holy Spirit. When I came up to the man, he was lying on the floor—curled up into a ball. It caught my attention that his extremities were becoming cold, to the point that his hands were turning blue. And his face was contorting. Clearly something unpleasant and demonic was happening, but I did not feel I had enough discernment to pray properly. I decided to do what I call "leaning in": I prayed for more of the Holy Spirit's anointing and power and presence to come upon the young man. Desperate situations require desperate measures, and I wanted to see him set free. So with authority, I also spoke to the hindrance that was keeping this man in bondage, directing it to identify itself.

Suddenly, even though the young man did not speak any English, he opened his mouth and said in clear, unaccented English, "Take the book out."

The what? I did not need a translator to understand the words, but I still did not know what he could be referring to. The man's body remained all contorted and curled up. I felt led to turn him onto his side to see if there was a book in his pocket, and sure enough, I found one—a copy of Hitler's *Mein Kampf.* After I took it out, his whole body relaxed, and he appeared to be relieved.

As it turned out, the man was a student from Hungary, and he was studying Communism at a university in Sarajevo. Apparently, when

I took the book out, the demons left him—they flat-out fled. Then the young man immediately got saved and even baptized in the Holy Spirit. He could not stop saying, "Your God Jesus! My God Jesus!" in Hungarian. (Interpreted for me into English.)

As you can see, receiving discernment in the situation made it possible to get rid of the unknown hindrance to freedom and salvation. I received only enough information to do what needed to happen. I never found out what the evil spirits were, nor did I discover how they came to control the fellow. There was no real dialogue between me and the young man—there was no time for it in such a setting and given the language barrier. I did know that the hindrance to his freedom emanated from a book in his possession and that it had to do with a spirit of antichrist. A collision of powers was occurring, and my part was to pray in the power of the gift of tongues, move in the gift of faith, and declare freedom in Jesus's name. It is often like that, although, as you will see in the next example, sometimes you are able to identify the evil spirit and determine more of its history with the person.

In this second situation, I was doing personal prayer counseling in a private setting. The man I was counseling told me he had been previously married to someone he initially thought was a wonderful woman, but who had left him for another man. It made no sense to him, and it broke his heart. He was a dedicated believer who seemed to have a lot going for him, but this turn of events had filled him with shame and condemnation. Now he had met someone else, but his sense of failure was keeping him from making a clear commitment. Something was in the way, and in our prayers we were trying to discern it.

This man could not believe that God would give him a second chance. He knew he had not done anything wrong (except to get deceived and beguiled in the first situation), but he could not stop carrying the sense of disillusionment, heartache, and shame. We tried several different approaches in prayer, but they didn't work. So, I started to sing praise songs softly, extolling Jesus's name.

Abruptly, I "knew in my knower" that the spirit of Jezebel was involved. This is a demonic entity named after the infamous, evil queen named Jezebel, wife of Ahab. (See 1 Kings 16:31; 18:13–19; 19:1–18; 21; 2 Kings 9:6–10, 30–37; Revelation 2:20.) I also "knew in my knower" that this demonic spirit had manipulated and deceived this man. (It is not that spirits have gender, but the Jezebel spirit is often associated with strong females who manipulate weak men such as Jezebel did Ahab.[24]) The evil spirit had initially beguiled this young man into a wrong relationship, and now he was all bound up inside as he approached a new relationship that lay within biblical boundaries.

Without saying anything out loud, I addressed the spirit silently. A noise like a freight train came roaring out of this good-looking young man. It was the demonic spirit or spirits of a Jezebelic nature. He was set free. The fruit of the discernment was freedom—and eventually a healthy, good marriage. The man was able to move forward, and in due time it was my honor to perform his wedding ceremony.

BE "QUICK OF SCENT"

Isaiah the prophet, foreseeing the ministry of Jesus as the Anointed One, declared that the Spirit of the Lord would *"make him of quick understanding* [literally, "quick of scent"] *in the fear of the LORD"* (Isaiah 11:3 KJV). In Scripture, the sense of smell operating independently of sight sometimes typifies the discernment that comes through the Holy Spirit.

For example, it is like being able to tell that what looks like a sheep is really a wolf in sheep's clothing. The human eye might not immediately discern anything amiss. But the nose of a sheep dog—which is much sharper than the human nose of a shepherd—is "quick of scent" to sound the alarm about the wolf.

Those to whom God commits the care of His sheep must likewise be godly sheepdogs through the Holy Spirit. They must be quick of scent, not judging by the evidence of their eyesight or their hearing or the reasoning of their natural minds, but rather sniffing out the

---

24. For more on this subject, see my book *Deliverance from Darkness* (Grand Rapids, MI: Chosen Books, 2010).

false prophets who have come among the people as wolves in sheep's clothing.

In fact, the sheepdog who neglects to bark when a wolf approaches has failed in his responsibility to the flock. As God said concerning Israel's watchmen (spiritual leaders) under the old covenant, *"They are all mute dogs"* (Isaiah 56:10). As a result of their failure, God's people became easy prey to their enemies. This not only happened in ancient Israel, but it has continued to happen in every generation up to the present. For our part, each one of us must learn to be quick of scent. Your little corner of God's flock needs you to be alert and prepared.

In part, I learned about the importance of being quick of scent from the great Bible teacher Derek Prince, who was a pioneer in ministries of deliverance, breaking curses, and the like. In the book *They Shall Expel Demons*, Derek Prince addresses the subject of characteristics of demonic activity: "We do not normally see them, but we recognize their presence by certain characteristic actions." He then lists their most typical activities, saying that demons entice, harass, torture, compel, enslave, cause addictions, defile, deceive, and attack the physical body.[25]

I learned an enormous amount from this statesman of the faith, including the importance of discerning when and where to confront the wolves in sheep's clothing. Some battles are mine, some are yours, some belong to someone else. Some need to be fought on the spot, some another day, some not at all. (Sometimes the enemy is trying to lure you into a dangerous and unnecessary conflict.) My book *Deliverance from Darkness* goes into much more detail about all of this.

Thus, throughout our lives, we must learn to be quick of scent—with accuracy and carefulness. In Christ Jesus, we are overcomers. But only on the condition that we follow Him wherever He leads us, deliberately and faithfully.

---

25. Derek Prince, *They Shall Expel Demons* (Grand Rapids, MI: Chosen Books, 1998), 165–166.

REACHING FOR A HIGHER REALM

Testing the spirits deals with all three aspects of discernment: revelation, interpretation, and application, although a different kind of spiritual filter needs to be applied to each aspect. I might pick up a revelation accurately only to interpret it incorrectly. Or I might get a revelation and its interpretation right, only to get stuck on the application (what I'm supposed to do with that information).

For example, let's say I get a revelation about a political situation, but it happens to touch on a sensitive area in my own experience. If I have hung on to bitterness, for example, my revelation will be tainted by my bitter opinion, which will render my revelation worthless to the kingdom of God. I need to be mindful of the influences that may come to bear on my thoughts and prayers and especially on the way I communicate. As I test the spirits around me, I need to include my own spirit, continually consulting with the Holy Spirit for guidance as to what to do.

This is why Romans 12 tells us to present our members to God as an acceptable act of worship, so we can "prove what the will of God is," what is *good and acceptable and perfect.*" (See Romans 12:1–2 NKJV.) God will help us identify our prejudices, whether they are personal, geographical, cultural, denominational, or whatever. If we present ourselves to Him, He will bring us into progressively greater cleansing. We will have less and less in common with the god of this world, and our own inner filter will become more effective. In other words, our progressive sanctification is just as important to our testing of the spirits as is our giftedness or our instruction in techniques.

Always remember, each one of us is supposed to learn to test the spirits; it is part of the Christian life!

> TESTING THE SPIRITS DEALS WITH
> ALL THREE ASPECTS OF DISCERNMENT:
> REVELATION, INTERPRETATION,
> AND APPLICATION.

PRAYER OF A DISCERNING HEART

Gracious Father, I thank You for Your great love. I want to be rooted and established in it. I declare that I trust in Your ability to lead and protect me more than I trust in the devil's power to deceive me. Furthermore, I declare that I have not received a spirit of fear, but power, love, and a sound mind. I choose to honor Your Word by examining everything in light of it and holding on to that which is good. I choose to honor those in authority over me, while asking that You sharpen my own capacity to grow in discernment from the Holy Spirit. Keep my feet firmly on Your path and my eyes clear with Your light. Without You, I am more helpless than an infant. With You, I am victorious over every enemy assault. I pray this in the name of Your Son Jesus. Amen.

8

THE SPIRIT OF DECEPTION: SEDUCTIVE AND MANIPULATIVE

*"The Spirit explicitly says that in later times
some will fall away from the faith, paying attention to deceitful
spirits and doctrines of demons."*
—1 Timothy 4:1 (NASB)

T o be forewarned is to be forearmed." That old saying captures a scriptural truth: discernment forewarns us so that we do not fall prey to subtle deceptions of the enemy. Forewarning gives us courage, too, as we find out what we are dealing with and what to do.

The above Scripture begins with the phrase, *"The Spirit explicitly says...."* The Holy Spirit is the one who forewarns us, in this case of the fact that some people will abandon their faith in Jesus because other attractions will draw them away; they will be allured by convincing voices that will manipulate their attention and cause them to give up on their belief. Their walk with the Lord will seem too wearisome and strenuous, and they will start to look for something more "fulfilling."

The *"later times"* referred to have been underway for centuries, and the warning still holds true for us today. These words were not written for unbelievers, but rather for full members of the church, and they expose the fact that it is easy to fall for the slick lies of the enemy even in a church setting.

However, the Spirit's warning in 1 Timothy 4 does not relegate to the trash heap those who fall away. It does not say that they cannot recover. (See verse 6.) It is not referring to the great apostasy of the end times. The warning comes with hope, conditional upon the response of those who heed it. We all need this word of warning because even if we never fall away ourselves, we will likely be aware of someone who does, and we may need to be able to discern what is going on so we can help that person out.

> DISCERNMENT FOREWARNS US
> SO THAT WE DO NOT FALL PREY TO
> SUBTLE DECEPTIONS OF THE ENEMY.

NAMES REVEAL THE NATURE

The Spirit's warning will be more effective for us if we understand the specific natures of the likely deceptions, and the best way to understand them is to know the names of the evil spirits involved. As Francis Frangipane states, "In the spirit realm the *name* of an entity always corresponds to its *nature*."[26]

The nature of a spiritual entity can be either positive or negative, as we will see in the various Scriptures throughout this section. First, here are a couple of examples of names that reveal God's divine nature:

> So Abraham called that place The Lord Will Provide. And to this day it is said, "On the mountain of the Lord it will be provided." (Genesis 22:14)

---

26. Francis Frangipane, *Discerning of Spirits* (Cedar Rapids, IA: Arrow Publications, 1994), 18, emphasis added.

*God said to Moses, "I AM WHO I AM. This is what you are to say
to the Israelites: 'I AM has sent me to you.'"* (Exodus 3:14)

We know God by many compound names found throughout
Scripture, such as *Jehovah Rapha* (The Lord Who Heals), *Jehovah Jireh*
(The Lord Who Provides), *Jehovah Nissi* (The Lord Our Banner), and
Jehovah Tsidkenu (The Lord Our Righteousness), not to mention the
titles King of Kings, Alpha and Omega, the Word, and many, many
more. Each name highlights an important aspect of His nature, thus
enabling us to know Him, trust Him, and live by faith.

By the same principle, if we can name demonic, or unclean, spirits,
we can better understand their nature and motivations and thus be
more effective in resisting their specific evil deceptions. Even the term
"unclean" spirit describes the nature of demonic beings. It is used in
Scripture both generically, as in *"I will also cause the prophets and the
unclean spirit to depart from the land"* (Zechariah 13:2 NKJV), and spe-
cifically, as in *"[Jesus] rebuked the unclean spirit, saying to it, 'You deaf
and mute spirit, I command you, come out of him and do not enter him
again'"* (Mark 9:25 NASB).[27]

In the account of the deliverance of the Gadarene demoniac in
Mark 5:6–9, the name "Legion" reveals the nature of the demonic
force being dealt with: *"for we are many."*

Another explicit example comes from the last book of the Bible:
*"They have as king over them, the angel of the abyss; his name in Hebrew
is Abaddon, and in the Greek he has the name Apollyon"* (Revelation
9:11 NASB). In English, the translation of *Abaddon* is "Destruction,"
and *Apollyon* means "Destroyer." As Jesus said of the Evil One, *"The
thief does not come except to steal, and to kill, and to destroy"* (John 10:10
NKJV).

A good part of discernment is understanding the nature of what
is being discerned, and names help us to lay hold of that knowledge.

---

27. See also Matthew 12:43–45; Mark 1:23–26; 3:30; 5:2–8; 7:25–30; Luke 8:27–35;
9:42; 11:24–26; Revelation 18:2.

WALKING THE BALANCE BEAM

Followers of Jesus Christ must continually maintain their spiritual balance by keeping their eyes on Him. The moment we turn our attention to the side, our steps weave and waver. If we try to follow anything or anybody but God, we can get off the narrow track altogether, and it takes a lot of effort to get back where we belong.

Thus, we are able to walk in a straight line only if we focus our attention on Christ, following the Lamb step-by-step as He leads us: *"These are the ones who follow the Lamb wherever He goes"* (Revelation 14:4 NKJV). At His personal invitation, we are followers of Christ, no longer followers of the devil:

> Then [Jesus] *said to* [Peter and Andrew], *"Follow Me, and I will make you fishers of men." They immediately left their nets and followed Him....* [Jesus] *called* [James and John], *and immediately they left the boat and their father, and followed Him.*
> (Matthew 4:19–20, 21–22 NKJV)

> As Jesus went on from there, He saw a man called Matthew, sitting in the tax collector's booth; and He said to him, "Follow Me!" And he got up and followed Him.   (Matthew 9:9 NASB)

> A large crowd followed [Jesus], and he healed all who were ill.... The crowds followed him on foot from the towns.
> (Matthew 12:15; 14:13)

Please join me in declaring our intention to follow the Lamb wherever He may lead us, and to turn our eyes away from distractions that would lead us astray.

DECEITFUL SPIRITS LURK IN THE SHADOWS

Even as we follow the Lord faithfully, deceitful unclean spirits are always lurking in the shadows, looking for some way to dissuade us from following Him. We need to be on our guard at all times. We can count on the Holy Spirit to help us discern and detect the presence of enemy spirits. The brilliant light of heaven not only shines like a beacon to guide us, but it also exposes whatever is hiding in the darkness. By this light, we can both discern deceitful spirits and elude their manipulations as we pursue the one true God.

We can find references to God's light throughout the Bible. Here are some examples from the New Testament:

The night is nearly over; the day is almost here. So let us put aside the deeds of darkness and put on the armor of light.
(Romans 13:12)

You are all children of the light and children of the day. We do not belong to the night or to the darkness. (1 Thessalonians 5:5)

Don't be deceived, my dear brothers and sisters. Every good and perfect gift is from above, coming down from the Father of the heavenly lights, who does not change like shifting shadows.
(James 1:16–17)

The deceitful spirits who lie in wait in the dark shadows aim to deflect God's people from the right path. Their insinuations are deceptive, manipulative, seductive, alluring. Demons lure people from a position of stability into instability in an attempt to capture them in their web of lies. Let us therefore always seek to *"walk in the light, as* [Jesus] *is in the light"* (1 John 1:7), "[putting] *on the armor of light"* as we learn to discern and dispel the workings of evil spirits.

WE CAN COUNT ON THE HOLY SPIRIT
TO HELP US DISCERN AND DETECT
THE PRESENCE OF ENEMY SPIRITS.

HOW DO EVIL SPIRITS DECEIVE?

Exposing and resisting the workings of demonic spirits involves recognizing the various tactics of the enemy. What methods do evil spirits use to deceive? They operate in different ways in different circumstances, perpetrating error in the most advantageous way possible by using a number of strategies, such as the following.

BY EXAGGERATION—TRUTH WRAPPED IN A LIE

Much of the seductiveness of the enemy's lies comes from the fact that they contain a kernel of truth. "You are sad, aren't you?" he may whisper to you. "You will never get over that thing your brother did to you. It's really affecting your personality. Why not do something about it? Why not get even with him, hmmm?"

It is true that your brother did something hurtful to you. It is true that you are sad. But the rest is an exaggeration and the beginning of an accusation. Soon a supposed truth is ringing in your head, and you lose sight of the real Truth. The insinuation provokes in you a desire to retaliate. You may have begun the day as a faithful follower of God, only to end it off in the weeds.

Paul was exasperated with the people of the church in Galatia because they fell for this trick of the devil, in which truth is mingled with falsehood. He wrote, "*O foolish Galatians! Who has bewitched you that you should not obey the truth…? … Are you so foolish? Having begun in the Spirit, are you now being made perfect by the flesh?*" (Galatians 3:1, 3 NKJV). To avoid being deceived in the same way, we must heed Paul's advice to "*demolish arguments and every pretension that sets itself up against the knowledge of God, and…take captive every thought to make it obedient to Christ*" (2 Corinthians 10:5).

BY EXALTING A SPECIAL REVELATION ABOVE THE WORD OF GOD

Uh-oh. This is a tricky one for people who are zealous to know God's revelation. If they do not watch out, they start holding the latest prophetic word higher than the written Word of God.

"That was revealed to him by an angel, so it must be reliable!"

"The Bible can't cover everything; that's why God sends extra-special revelation like this."

"Get outta my way! Personal experiences don't lie!"

Obviously, I believe that God does send special revelation to His people—but never, ever should it be held in higher esteem than the Scriptures. Even though I myself have had a number of angelic visitations and supernatural experiences that are almost indescribable, I want to remain open to correction at all times, and I return to the "main and plain" message of Scripture all the time. The extras are just extra. My happiness, and especially my salvation, do not depend on them. God helping me, I will always take seriously these warnings of Paul to the believers under his care:

> Do not let anyone who delights in false humility and the worship of angels disqualify you. Such a person also goes into great detail about what they have seen; they are puffed up with idle notions by their unspiritual mind. They have lost connection with the head, from whom the whole body, supported and held together by its ligaments and sinews, grows as God causes it to grow.
> (Colossians 2:18–19)

> I am astonished that you are so quickly deserting the one who called you to live in the grace of Christ and are turning to a different gospel—which is really no gospel at all. Evidently some people are throwing you into confusion and are trying to pervert the gospel of Christ. But even if we or an angel from heaven should preach a gospel other than the one we preached to you, let them be under God's curse! As we have already said, so now I say again: If anybody is preaching to you a gospel other than what you accepted, let them be under God's curse! (Galatians 1:6–9)

People too easily fall for the appeal of an exciting new message or its messenger, or they begin to say, "Oh well, if I can hear God for myself, then I don't have to pay as much attention to God's Word and to what I already know to be true, because now I can just listen, and He's going to direct me." They may even back up this approach with a proof text such as this one: *"Your ears will hear a word behind you, 'This is the way, walk in it,' whenever you turn to the right or to the left"* (Isaiah 30:21 NASB). But remember that the Holy Spirit never contradicts God's Word, and that we need both the written Word and special revelation. Moreover, to be discerning, we must consider the whole of God's revelation in the Scriptures and not just focus on isolated parts.

At times, we become more susceptible to deception if we are feeling desperate about something. For example, we may so badly want healing or some kind of miracle for ourselves or for someone else that we will cling to a "word" we have heard that did not originate with God. In this way, our emotional weak spots become entry points for the enemy's alluring, fraudulent messages.

This is a slippery slope. One mild-sounding deception can lead to worse ones. How else do you think people end up in cults or seriously off-balance? Again, to maintain our spiritual balance, we must learn to measure our experiences, emotions, and any special revelation by the authority of God's written Word.

> TO BE DISCERNING, WE MUST CONSIDER THE WHOLE OF GOD'S REVELATION IN THE SCRIPTURES AND NOT JUST FOCUS ON ISOLATED PARTS.

BY PRIDEFUL SELF-PROMOTION

Another way the devil loves to deceive people is by persuading them that they are better than others. Even though the Bible says clearly, "Do not forsake the assembling of believers" (see Hebrews 10:25), such people may become convinced that they are too big (too elite, too important, more educated, above criticism) to fellowship with "ordinary" Christians in an "ordinary" church. They position themselves above accountability to anyone else, exalting their own giftedness or experience level.

Or they may buy into some trend in the church, even a genuine move of the Spirit, and make their association with it a source of personal pride. Eventually, they can become what I call "parked cars" in a cul-de-sac of yesterday's move of God. They have not moved forward with the Holy Spirit. Neither have they reached out to others with God's love.

The only cure is humility and accountability. I saw this process at work back when I was part of the "Kansas City Prophets" fellowship and we were accused of all sorts of aberrant practices. I do not think we felt we were all that elite, but some of the people who followed us did, and an international uproar broke out in 1990 from the heartland of America. Fame can be so intoxicating and potentially dangerous. But frankly, knowing everything behind the scenes, I was very impressed with the way Mike Bickle, the senior leader of Kansas City Fellowship, handled the accusations. Time after time, he responded with humility, acknowledging mistakes and attempting to set things right. In the long run, it opened the way for a lot of healthy adjustments and maturing in wisdom in prophetic development in Kansas City and elsewhere. *"God opposes the proud but shows favor to the humble"* (James 4:6, quoting Proverbs 3:34).

THROUGH HERO WORSHIP

Another subtle deception of the enemy is hero worship. Along comes a preacher with a golden tongue, and blessings accrue to him. Soon he has a ministry, a slot on television or radio, and a new wardrobe. When he goes on the speaking circuit, people flock to hear him and, if they can get close enough, to take selfies with him.

It is the people I am concerned about, because hero worship has a way of taking worship away from the only one it belongs to, God Himself, and this leads people away from the truth. That's what happened with some of the followers of William Branham, the successful healing evangelist before World War II. He was truly highly gifted by

God and marvelously used in the detailed gift of a word of knowledge and so much more. But sadly, certain of his followers elevated him to the position of "the Elijah," saying that he had returned as "the forerunner" before the second coming of Jesus.

Please hear me, this man was called and anointed by God. But some people declared him to be someone he was not. Even to this day, a remnant gathers at his graveside on a particular day of the year in hopes that he will return. This shows how people's honor and respect for someone can become distorted and end up developing into dangerous cultish hero worship.

We have had too much of this in church history. So watch out when you see someone drawing too much attention to themselves or to gifts and experiences; exercise discernment when you see people begin to hero-worship a leader or speaker. Such things can happen again and they will. There is nothing new under the sun.

> *The Spirit expressly says that in latter times some will depart from the faith, giving heed to deceiving spirits and doctrines of demons, speaking lies in hypocrisy, having their own conscience seared with a hot iron....* (1 Timothy 4:1–2 NKJV)

HERO WORSHIP HAS A WAY OF TAKING WORSHIP AWAY FROM THE ONLY ONE IT BELONGS TO, GOD HIMSELF, AND THIS LEADS PEOPLE AWAY FROM THE TRUTH.

THE TRUTH WILL SET YOU FREE

In his book *Let No One Deceive You*, scholar and theologian Dr. Michael Brown gives us encouragement for guarding against deception:

According to the New Testament, the possibility of deception is very real. But that does not mean that everyone has to be deceived! We can be kept safe in Jesus. The Lord can bring us into a wide place where we can be firmly rooted and secure, and it is for that very reason the Bible often says to us: "Be not deceived."[28]

Beloved, let's learn to walk in humility and with gratitude, letting the peace of Christ rule in our hearts. (See Colossians 3:15.) Let's walk in accountability. Let's honor the Word of God. Let's know the truth, because the truth will set us free! (See John 8:31–32.)

REACHING FOR A HIGHER REALM

Paul wrote, *"And this I pray, that your love may abound still more and more in real knowledge and all discernment"* (Philippians 1:9 NASB). The noblest use of our discernment is to allow it to enlighten the love that God pours into our hearts. Then we will walk in a spirit opposite to self-glorification and pride.

God gives us grace to live in His love: *"For the grace of God has appeared that offers salvation to all people. It teaches us to say 'No' to ungodliness and worldly passions, and to live self-controlled, upright and godly lives in this present age"* (Titus 2:11–12). You can regain your place in that grace if you've strayed from it, but only if you surrender your independent claim to know what is right. *"For in Him [Jesus Christ] all the fullness of Deity dwells in bodily form, and in Him you have been made complete, and He is the head over all rule and authority"* (Colossians 2:9–10 NASB).

I want to be a person who starts well by grace—and who also finishes well by grace in true love, knowledge, and discernment. Don't you?

---

28. Michael Brown, *Let No One Deceive You* (Shippensburg, PA: Destiny Image, 1997), 61.

PRAYER OF A DISCERNING HEART

Gracious Father, in Jesus's mighty name I pray, thanking You for the light of Your Word. I admit my total dependency upon You. Shine Your light on me. If there is any form of deception in my life, I ask Your Spirit to send conviction, revelation, discernment, and freedom. Help me to respond well to You and to extend Your grace to my family and friends. I choose to revoke my alliance with any form of darkness and to step into proper alignment with Your ways. Guard me against further deception. Help me to pierce through the seductive lies of the enemy and grant me wisdom to apply Your truth. I ask that You would do exceedingly abundantly above all that I could ever ask or imagine, and that You would turn everything in my life to the good.

With a heart full of worship, I magnify Your great name. I rejoice in Your wonderful, complete salvation. Amen.

9

EXPOSING DEMONIC INFLUENCES: SETTING THE CAPTIVES FREE

"[Jesus] stood up to read, and the scroll of the prophet Isaiah was handed to him. Unrolling it, he found the place where it is written: 'The Spirit of the Lord is on me, because he has anointed me to proclaim good news to the poor. He has sent me to proclaim freedom for the prisoners and recovery of sight for the blind, to set the oppressed free, to proclaim the year of the Lord's favor.' Then he rolled up the scroll, gave it back to the attendant and sat down. The eyes of everyone in the synagogue were fastened on him."
—Luke 4:16–20

It was no surprise when Jesus stood up in His hometown synagogue on the Sabbath day to read the above passage from the prophet Isaiah—but nobody expected Him to make it personal: *"The Spirit of the Lord is on me...."*

Isaiah had prophesied about a Messiah who was to come in the distant future. Now, here was Jesus, essentially announcing to the dumbstruck congregation, "I am that Messiah." In case they didn't quite understand, He added, *"Today this scripture is fulfilled in your hearing"* (Luke 4:21).

Using Isaiah's words, He broadcasted His messianic job description. The townspeople must have wondered what He was talking about. What did He mean, "*freedom for the prisoners,*" "*recovery of sight for the blind,*" and "*set the oppressed free*"? What kind of bondage did He intend to break? "*Recovery of sight*" sounded like more than physical healing for blind people. And was this some kind of a political statement? Anyway, wasn't this just that guy Jesus, the son of Joseph the local carpenter?

To the people, it didn't make any sense.

DISCERNMENT AND DELIVERANCE

Today, we have a better idea of what Jesus meant, because most of us have experienced the freedom from bondage that He was talking about. We have realized that we were once slaves to sin and Satan, now set free from emotional, mental, and spiritual oppression. By accepting Jesus's offer of salvation, we have been liberated from the burdens of our unsaved, captive condition.

However, we seem to encounter an endless stream of hindrances to walking in complete personal freedom. We need Jesus's ongoing ministry of freedom in this "*year of the Lord's favor,*" as Isaiah puts it. The prophecy proclaims release to the captives and recovery of sight to the blind, yet too often we grope like blind men as we try to navigate the way of salvation. We need new eyes of discernment even to be able to identify the nature and degree of our past bondage and its lingering effects.

Additionally, only with God-given discernment can we tell apart the good and evil influences that surround us. We more often come up against what I call "demonic influences" than identifiable demons who have specific assignments against us. For example, when someone says, "There's an angry spirit in the nation," they are referring to a pervasive angry influence that cannot be cast out with a simple prayer for deliverance. The angry spirit is manifested in the demonically influenced words and deeds of people. This influence is a spiritual force that twists and taints and pollutes God's way of love. It is like a spider web, and people get stuck in it. Writhing in their captivity, they act out of a "web mentality"—and I'm not (necessarily) referring to the World Wide Web.

We Christians often cannot discern what is really going on. We cast blame right and left on a human level, failing to expose the demonic influences around us. We may even be part of the problem. Yet with the Spirit of Jesus Christ living inside us, we have both a responsibility to address demonic influences and the ability to do so. Jesus is still in the captive-freeing business today, right where you live.

I remember something that Mike Bickle said years ago when he and I were serving together in Kansas City. Even then, he was a leader. He was an intercessor and a revivalist, a strong teacher of the Word, a man of high standards. But he summarized his life purpose without defining himself in those ways. He said that God had called him to be "a worshipper of God and a deliverer of men, in that order." He was a worshipper of God first, a deliverer of men second. I trust that I am also. And I invite you to be the same.

"A worshipper of God and a deliverer of men"—we cannot have one without the other, and both aspects are meant to be fully activated in us. As we worship God and surrender ourselves to Him, He meets us with freedom. As we ask the Holy Spirit to cast His light on the hindrances that keep us from receiving and discerning His revelation and acting upon it, He answers our prayers and sets us free, and we are empowered to give away what we have received. Walking in a new spirit of freedom, we are able to share it with others.

> WE ARE TO BE "WORSHIPPERS OF GOD
> AND DELIVERERS OF MEN."

DISCERNING DEMONIC INFLUENCES

Let us now look at some of the major demonic influences working in the world today and how to counteract them.

THE RELIGIOUS SPIRIT

One of the greatest hindrances you will encounter in your Christian walk is "the religious spirit." Whole books have been written about the distinct patterns of behavior that distinguish the religious spirit, and I will only be able to touch on them here.

Rick Joyner, founder of MorningStar Ministries, defines a religious spirit as "a demon that seeks to substitute religious activity for the power of the Holy Spirit in our lives."[29] Religious spirits endeavor to interfere with the free flow of the Holy Spirit in the lives of believers. They can be hard to discern precisely because they are religious; they are pious, even hyper-spiritual. Their influence can pervade a person's life and church like yeast pervades a lump of dough. That's why Jesus said, *"Watch out and beware of the leaven of the Pharisees and Sadducees"* (Matthew 16:6 NASB).

In New Testament times, the Pharisees and Sadducees were the professional religionists. The Pharisees were the watchdogs of religious purity, chastising any Jewish person who transgressed even slightly, promoting the perfectionistic performance of their strict interpretation of the requirements of the law of Moses. The Pharisees and Sadducees did not agree with each other in the details of what constituted true religion, and they competed with each other in zeal. Each held to *"a form of godliness, although they…denied its power"* (2 Timothy 3:5 NASB).

Generally, the religious spirit promotes a works-based or performance-based lifestyle. The main message is, "You're not good enough; try harder." Although the cross of Jesus has made performance-based religion a thing of the past, the religious spirit likes to keep it alive so that people will labor under a triple burden of guilt, fear, and pride. Every person on earth rightfully seeks a sense of acceptance, but the religious spirit keeps the ultimate acceptance—God's—just out of reach.

---

29. Rick Joyner, *Overcoming Evil in the Last Days* (Shippensburg, PA: Destiny Image, 2003), 130.

The religious spirit is active in the church today; sadly, many churches and ministries are characterized by it. In such an environment, discipleship consists of mastering a list of do's and don'ts, often along with unhealthy one-upmanship: How many books of the Bible have you read? Have you memorized more verses than the average person? Do you read the "right" Bible version? Were you baptized properly? How rich is your prayer life? Do you fast regularly? Do you tithe? Et cetera.

Now, that doesn't mean that most of these activities aren't good things; they are. It is the *spirit* behind the attitudes and the demands about them that are twisted. You and I do not need to earn brownie points with God. Jesus doesn't grade on a curve. By His death and resurrection, Christ Jesus has secured our acceptance with the Father once and for all as we place our faith in Him.

Yet when we live and breathe in an environment tainted by the religious spirit, it is difficult for us to discern that we're being affected by a demonic influence. I know that God can set us free from it, though. (See Philippians 1:6.) I remember something my oldest son once said when he came home from California for a visit. He had been away from home for a while. The family was sitting around the table, talking and having some fun. Suddenly, he said, "Dad? I like this rendition of you a whole lot better than the former one. When did you get delivered of that religious spirit?"

> THE RELIGIOUS SPIRIT CAUSES
> PEOPLE TO LABOR UNDER A TRIPLE BURDEN
> OF GUILT, FEAR, AND PRIDE.

Wow! I had not done anything purposely; I didn't even know I was acting differently. But I had been partaking deeply of a new outpouring of the Holy Spirit. Evidently, the more saturated with the Spirit I became, the more my old shackles fell off. Some of my uptightness had to do with my background and upbringing, and some had come from what I had been taught as an adult believer. But the powerful presence of the Holy Spirit had prevailed over the religious spirit. I was definitely less rigid than before and less afraid of failure and rejection. Of course I was more joyful and fun to be with, too.

It is always easier to spot the religious spirit in someone else, and to judge them, than it is to recognize it in ourselves. As quick as I may be to perceive a religious spirit coming at me through another person, I am not as quick to recognize the same spirit when I look in the mirror. Seer prophet Bob Jones used to teach that you could tell when a person was moving into an overly religious mode of operation by looking for five telltale attitudes: legalism, criticism, debate, opinion, and judgment. Let's apply that measure to ourselves and take the log out of our own eyes instead of pointing out the splinters in others' eyes. (See, for example, Matthew 7:4–5.)

To repeat: guilt, fear, and pride are the earmarks of the religious spirit. A proud demeanor often masks the fearful, insecure soul of someone who is trying desperately to make the grade. Yet looking for security within oneself just perpetuates the anxiety, because self-centered security is such a poor substitute for God-centered security.

Many insecure people become perfectionists. They cannot rest; it is as though they are shackled to a treadmill. I don't know about you, but I want to stay out of that rat race. I know that God wants me to strive for excellence, but I also know I cannot do it in my own strength. I need God's grace to shine where I am weak. That will make more of an impact for the kingdom than my perfectionism ever would, and it may result in deliverance for other people, too. As Paul wrote, "[The Lord] *said to me, 'My grace is sufficient for you, for my power is made perfect in weakness.' Therefore I will boast all the more gladly about my weaknesses, so that Christ's power may rest on me*" (2 Corinthians 12:9).

THE POLITICAL SPIRIT

The religious spirit is often allied with the political spirit. This coalition has occurred in every age and in every culture. It can be seen in the case of the Pharisees, who joined with political forces to achieve their purpose of discrediting and eliminating Jesus. Look what happened even at the start of Jesus's ministry: *"The Pharisees went out and immediately began conspiring with the Herodians against Him, as to how they might destroy Him"* (Mark 3:6 NASB). Three years later, when Jesus was arrested and taken into custody, He was passed back and forth between the religious and political leaders.

Jesus understood what was happening, but He did not resist, choosing to let the evil seem to prevail because God's greater purposes were at work for the salvation of the world. *"Jesus gave [Herod] no answer. The chief priests and the teachers of the law were standing there, vehemently accusing him. Then Herod and his soldiers ridiculed and mocked him"* (Luke 23:9–11). Jesus's disciples did not understand what was going on; to them, the situation seemed like a disaster, and they did not discern the demonic forces at play. When a political spirit is running the show, you cannot recognize its hidden agendas with your natural senses. They have to be spiritually discerned.

In his landmark book, *The Political Spirit*, Faisal Malick gives one the best summaries I have read of the goal and mode of operation of this demonic entity:

> The political spirit has been specifically assigned to block the establishment of the government of the Kingdom of God on the earth by instituting false government and corrupt political practices. It's the spirit behind the positioning and strife we see in earthly governments and behind divisions in the Church.[30]

The political spirit is an invisible demonic mastermind that strategizes ways to thwart God's plans; to achieve its corrupt goals, it enters into alliances with religious spirits and institutions backed by mammon. The political spirit will always try to buy off, corrupt, manipulate, and dominate leaders and groups of people. It mesmerizes people into false loyalties while issuing demands of uniformity

30. Faisal Malick, *The Political Spirit* (Shippensburg, PA: Destiny Image, 2008), 13.

through the pressures of fear, shame, and control. Again, religion plays a major role.

In addition to the circumstances surrounding Jesus's arrest and crucifixion, we see numerous examples throughout history of the coalition of the political spirit and the religious spirit: the Crusades, for instance, or the many religious wars and skirmishes that have been fought over the centuries. Without much difficulty, we can discern the same influences today in many levels of conflict, from wars of political rhetoric to terrorist activities.

Particularly in these days of instant social messaging, we need to be alert to the influence of the political spirit around us. We have to work hard to keep our focus on God and not on the troubling and divisive contemporary issues unfolding around us, lest we react to them by joining the toxic fray rather than being part of the solution. While we should fulfill our civic responsibilities and keep a level head while participating in our representative government, the best thing we can do is to pray and intercede in order to break the power of the demonic political spirit that causes divisions, animosity, and strife. *"For our struggle is not against flesh and blood, but against the rulers, against the authorities, against the powers of this dark world and against the spiritual forces of evil in the heavenly realms"* (Ephesians 6:12).

THE SPIRIT OF FEAR AND INTIMIDATION

Another demonic hindrance falls under the category of fear and intimidation. It is the direct opposite of the spirit that God gives us: *"For God has not given us a spirit of fear, but of power and of love and of a sound mind"* (2 Timothy 1:7 NKJV).

Fear is a demonic specialty. With fear and intimidation, Satan holds people captive, controlling them with threats of dire consequences. For example, the spirit of fear and intimidation will threaten a pastor, saying, "You watch out. If you speak up about the truth, you will lose your license to preach. You will be excommunicated." It influences people to keep safe under low ceilings and to stay with the opinion of the crowd. At times, it entices people into sexual or financial sin in order to brand them a failure and fill them with shame and guilt.

The spirit of fear and intimidation works closely with both the religious spirit and the political spirit. Together, these evil spirits demean people and preoccupy them with their own inadequacies so that they won't focus on God's love, the empowerment of the Holy Spirit, and the finished work of the cross of the Lord Jesus on their behalf.

Diabolic powers drive you with angry whips—whereas Jesus, the Good Shepherd, *leads* you. Jesus reserves His aggression for the demonic enemies that He fights on our behalf. With God on our side, we will be the victors, just as the men of Israel were under Joshua:

> *So it was, when they brought out those kings to Joshua, that Joshua called for all the men of Israel, and said to the captains of the men of war who went with him, "Come near, put your feet on the necks of these kings." And they drew near and put their feet on their necks. Then Joshua said to them, "Do not be afraid, nor be dismayed; be strong and of good courage, for thus the LORD will do to all your enemies against whom you fight."*
>
> (Joshua 10:24–25 NKJV)

> EVIL SPIRITS PREOCCUPY PEOPLE WITH THEIR INADEQUACIES SO THEY WON'T FOCUS ON GOD'S LOVE, THE HOLY SPIRIT'S EMPOWERMENT, AND JESUS' FINISHED WORK ON THE CROSS ON THEIR BEHALF.

Fear will paralyze you, but faith will propel you forward to victory and freedom. The victory is lasting. My late wife proved it. She was always a wonderful person, but she used to be timid about speaking out and taking initiative. Then she had a powerful experience that drew her into a prolonged season of intimacy with God. In the midst of it, she was delivered of spirits of fear and rejection and people-pleasing.

She bloomed into the person she was meant to be. Instead of seeking approval for everything, she boldly began to wear a baseball cap backwards that had the words "No More Fear" written on it. On the inside of the bill it read, "Don't let your fears stand in the way of your dreams."

THE SPIRIT OF ANTICHRIST

The spirit of antichrist is indeed active in the world today, using its influence as we move toward the final day of the Lord:

> *Dear children, this is the last hour; and as you have heard that the antichrist is coming, even now many antichrists have come. This is how we know it is the last hour. They went out from us, but they did not really belong to us. For if they had belonged to us, they would have remained with us; but their going showed that none of them belonged to us.* (1 John 2:18–19)

Do not let this particular demonic hindrance throw you due to its name. The "spirit of antichrist" refers collectively to all evil spirits who oppose Christ by trying to supplant Him. Refusing to honor the fact that He is God's Anointed One, these spirits promote false anointings to make people set themselves up as superior in order to deflect worship and devotion away from Jesus Christ.

The spirit of antichrist works alongside the other demonic influences to try to weaken the kingdom of God. But there is a simple scriptural test that helps us expose the spirit of antichrist:

> *This is how you can recognize the Spirit of God: Every spirit that acknowledges that Jesus Christ has come in the flesh is from God, but every spirit that does not acknowledge Jesus is not from God. This is the spirit of the antichrist, which you have heard is coming and even now is already in the world.* (1 John 4:2–3)

The false anointing of the spirit of antichrist is convincing and persuasive. People are fooled by it. It is almost unprecedented to see this lie exposed publicly. However, that is what happened in the case of the Worldwide Church of God of California. Under the domination of founder Herbert W. Armstrong, this cult spread its influence and spawned controversy for decades in the twentieth century. Sensational pronouncements and aberrant doctrines took the place of solid discipleship. But when Armstrong died in 1986, his appointed successor, Joseph W. Tkach, surprised everybody by leading a revolutionary doctrinal reversal that eventually resulted in the denomination's acceptance into the National Association of Evangelicals. Many of their substantial real estate holdings were sold off, including the Ambassador Auditorium in Pasadena, which is now owned by HRock Church, pastored by my dear friend Ché Ahn and his son, Gabe Ahn.

Likewise, as people with God's discernment who pursue the things of God with passion, we must be vigilant against unscriptural claims and false anointings, always returning to the safety check of the Word of God and the lordship of Jesus Christ.

REACHING FOR A HIGHER REALM

Being able to identify elusive demonic influences is only the beginning. What will you do with what you discern? Should you become some kind of whistle-blower? And how can you resist the pull of evil yourself while helping to deliver others from deception? Run the other way?

In his book *The Three Battlegrounds*, Francis Frangipane breaks spiritual warfare down into three primary fronts: your own mind, the church, and the wider unseen supernatural reality. Only after you discern a demonic influence in your own life and conquer it in the power of Jesus Christ can you advance to the next battleground or sphere of authority, which is your local church and perhaps the larger church. Eventually, you may earn enough authority to effectively handle your part of the battle on the worldwide front.

Frangipane writes about "following the Lamb wherever He goes,"[31] which, by implication, refers to walking in the opposite spirit from that of the demonic entities. He also writes,

---

31. Francis Frangipane, *The Three Battlegrounds* (Cedar Rapids, IA: Arrow Publications, 1989, 2006), 66.

The spirit of antichrist is a world ruler (see Ephesians 6:12). It cannot be cast out as a lesser demon might. Ultimate victory over all such principalities comes through *displacement*, where the encouragement and love of Christ floods the thought-life of the local Christian community. As we become the opposite of antichrist, we will see Christ's body healed, and the spirit of antichrist trodden under our feet.[32]

You can walk in this "opposite spirit" to combat all demonic influences, including the religious spirit, the political spirit, the spirit of fear and intimidation, and the spirit of antichrist. It is hard not to stumble at times, though. In order to keep walking in the opposite spirit, you may need various kinds of assistance (including outright deliverance from the influence of specific evil spirits) and scriptural counseling. Since walking in the opposite spirit entails walking closely with the Spirit of Jesus, you can count on Him to show you the way. As you advance along this way, the demonic spirits of this world will have less and less in common with you, to the degree that you can eventually say, as Jesus did, *"The prince of this world is coming. He has no hold over me"* (John 14:30).

May the Holy Spirit grant light to each of us. May we not point the finger in judgment, saying, "Oh, that demonic spirit is operating in our church leadership," or "I see a territorial spirit over our city"— until we have let the Holy Spirit clean house in our own lives so we can exercise clear discernment. May the Spirit bring us into such a thorough understanding of the ways of God that we will have nothing in common with the religious spirit, the political spirit, the spirit of fear and intimidation, and the spirit of antichrist. The Lord Himself is our refuge from all such demonic influences:

If you say, "The LORD is my refuge," and you make the Most High your dwelling, no harm will overtake you.... ... "Because he loves me," says the LORD, "I will rescue him; I will protect him, for he acknowledges my name. He will call on me, and I will answer him;

---

32. Ibid., 122, emphasis added.

I will be with him in trouble, I will deliver him and honor him."
(Psalm 91:9–10, 14–15)

PRAYER OF A DISCERNING HEART

Heavenly Father, in Jesus's name, I worship You and enthrone You with my praises. According to Your Word, Jesus came to set the captives free and to declare *"the year of the Lord's favor."* As an ambassador of Christ, I believe the Holy Spirit has anointed me to be a worshipper of God and a deliverer of men. Once again, I surrender to You all that I am and all that I hope to be. Anoint me with a higher level of discernment so I can know the motivation of the spirit behind an activity. By the grace of God, I believe that I am receiving an increase of Your revelatory ways in my life. For Your kingdom's sake, amen.

10

STAYING OUT OF SATAN'S TRAPS: WISDOM FOR AVOIDING COMMON PITFALLS

"For such men are false apostles, deceitful workers, disguising themselves as apostles of Christ. No wonder, for even Satan disguises himself as an angel of light. Therefore it is not surprising if his servants also disguise themselves as servants of righteousness, whose end will be according to their deeds."
—2 Corinthians 11:13–15 (NASB)

My late wife, Michal Ann, once ministered at a women's conference in France. In order to bring home an important point, she asked the women to come to the next morning's session *without* putting on their makeup. This was an especially relevant exercise to do in France, a land filled with beautiful women who love their cosmetics. Michal Ann wanted them to grasp the fact that each one of them was beautiful to Jesus the Beloved regardless of her outward appearance.

It worked. The simple act of showing up without makeup for public worship and fellowship brought deliverance to a number of women. They went home feeling loved and liberated. Most of them went back to wearing makeup the next day, but they were forever changed inside.

They had discovered that they were wholly acceptable and even desirable to God without the "beauty masks" that they usually wore.

I am not a woman, but I can imagine that those women felt cleaner and more authentic after that day. By one simple action, they had redefined themselves, and they had clambered out of one of the common traps that Satan sets for God's people—all of which seem to relate to the false fronts set up by our human pride.

COMMON SATANIC PITFALLS

As we know, Satan has established an evil spiritual kingdom as a rival to God's kingdom. He rules over fallen angels and demonic spirits and incites them to seek to establish footholds in our minds and hearts. Here are some common Satanic pitfalls that we need to both discern and avoid.

DISGUISES AND MASQUERADE PARTIES

In the passage from 2 Corinthians at the beginning of this chapter, the word *disguise* is used three times in various forms. Other translations use "*masquerade*" or similar terms. In addition, Paul used the words "*false*" and "*deceitful*." I think maybe he was trying to make a point, don't you? He was warning us against status-seeking people within the church who claim to be more anointed and righteous than they really are, who masquerade as men and women of strength and integrity but who are nothing like that if you scratch the surface.

Falseness and deceit are part of the fallen human condition. Centuries before Paul's time, God addressed the same issue, speaking through the prophet Isaiah:

> "*Because this people draw near with their words and honor Me with their lip service, but they remove their hearts far from Me, and their reverence for Me consists of tradition learned by rote, therefore behold, I will once again deal marvelously with this people, wondrously marvelous; and the wisdom of their wise men will perish, and the discernment of their discerning men will be*

concealed." *Woe to those who deeply hide their plans from the* LORD, *and whose deeds are done in a dark place, and they say,* *"Who sees us?" or "Who knows us?"*   (Isaiah 29:13–15 NASB)

Believers who begin to live behind a false front soon lose their discernment. It happens with the shifting of their boundaries between truth and error. As soon as a person sees that they have managed to fool others—and the first time often feels so good—the boundaries of their conscience begin to shift. Truth becomes a relative thing. They reason their way into more deception without realizing what they're doing.

God is light and the source of light—and Satan disguises himself as an angel of light. Satan is the original imitator. He presents a falsified and distorted version of God's truth and tempts us to do the same. The enemy motivates high-seeming mannerisms while reinforcing low-level manners. In short, he puts on a big masquerade party.

There are apparent rewards for moving into pretense—adulation from others, position, power. But once a person puts on a disguise and begins to pretend to be someone else, pride gains a foothold, even becoming arrogance or hubris. It may not be all that obvious to other people. Possibly because so many of us are two-faced, it seems normal; we think nothing of it when someone acts one way in public and another way in private. We accept hypocrisy in ourselves and others.

> BELIEVERS WHO BEGIN TO LIVE BEHIND
> A FALSE FRONT SOON LOSE THEIR
> DISCERNMENT. IT HAPPENS WITH
> THE SHIFTING OF THEIR BOUNDARIES
> BETWEEN TRUTH AND ERROR.

The word *hypocrite* comes from the Greek word for "actor," but in no way is our life in Christ supposed to be a performance. Instead, it is a life of stripping off our masks and behaving with loving humility.

The only way we can discern good from evil and light from dark is to reject our role-playing and to be so in tune with the real truth and source of light that, as a result, we can see, hear, feel, taste, smell, and know the difference. God's light exposes the darkness. When we walk closely with the Holy Spirit, He helps us to detect disguises in ourselves and others, and He shows us how to be set free. He will enable us to distinguish the true light from the false version.

THE SPIRIT OF LEVIATHAN (PRIDE)

We have discussed pride in several contexts in this book, but let's look at it from a further perspective. The *"twisted serpent"* Leviathan (Isaiah 27:1 NASB, NKJV) has come to represent the fierce pride of the enemy. Leviathan is about twisted communication. The spirit of Leviathan partners with the political spirit, the religious spirit, the antichrist spirit, and other spirits to twist the truth and to make it palatable to susceptible saints. Pride can also interfere with communication by preventing hearers from understanding what someone is trying to say. Additionally, pride causes offense and breeds fear and overreaction. Prideful Leviathan is a formidable foe indeed:

> *Can you pull in Leviathan with a fishhook or tie down its tongue with a rope? Can you put a cord through its nose or pierce its jaw with a hook? Will it keep begging you for mercy? Will it speak to you with gentle words? Will it make an agreement with you for you to take it as your slave for life? Can you make a pet of it like a bird or put it on a leash for the young women in your house? Will traders barter for it? Will they divide it up among the merchants? Can you fill its hide with harpoons or its head with fishing spears? If you lay a hand on it, you will remember the struggle and never do it again! Any hope of subduing it is false; the mere sight of it is overpowering. No one is fierce enough to rouse it. Who then is able to stand against me?* (Job 41:1–10)

> *In that day the LORD with His severe sword, great and strong, will punish Leviathan the fleeing serpent, Leviathan that twisted*

serpent; and He will slay the reptile that is in the sea.

(Isaiah 27:1 NKJV)

Accurate teaching about Leviathan is summarized on the back cover of the study guide to the book *Leviathan Exposed* by my dear friend and the associate leader of XP Ministries, Robert Hotchkin:

Leviathan is a high-level demonic spirit that works subtly behind the scenes to twist and pervert communications with the goal of destroying relationships and alliances. It wants to derail your destiny and infiltrate every area of your life—creating chaos, confusion, devastation, and destruction.[33]

As the Scriptures tell us, pride always comes before a fall: *"Pride goes before destruction, and a haughty spirit before a fall"* (Proverbs 16:18 NKJV). Yet sometimes it seems to take a long time for the fall to come. How does the Lord kill the dragon named Pride in us? The best way is for us to cooperate with Him in this process, allowing Him to search our hearts, so that the fall may be prevented and we can regain a clear spirit before Him. (See Psalm 139:23–24.)

> LET US COOPERATE WITH GOD TO KILL THE DRAGON NAMED PRIDE IN US, ALLOWING HIM TO SEARCH OUR HEARTS, SO THAT WE CAN REGAIN A CLEAR SPIRIT BEFORE HIM.

For example, when I purposefully draw closer to God, a spotlight begins to shine into the murky depths of my soul. Is that a serpent I see slithering by? Do I want him to stay? How can I stop harboring him and feeding him? How can I obtain even more of God's light to expose his slippery schemes? I pray, "Send Your light and grace, Lord!

33. Robert Hotchkin, *Leviathan Exposed Study Guide* (Maricopa, AZ: XP Publishing, 2016), back cover.

I humble myself before You. Help! I cannot help myself." *"But he gives us more grace. That is why Scripture says: 'God opposes the proud but shows favor to the humble'"* (James 4:6).

Leviathan and his kin may return another day to tempt me into more prideful, twisted thinking, but I can be set free by calling on God in unpretentious humility, once more taking the clear advice of Scripture: *"Yes, all of you be submissive to one another, and be clothed with humility, for 'God resists the proud, but gives grace to the humble'"* (1 Peter 5:5 NKJV). God always shows grace-filled favor to the humble. This is the opposite of the fear and intimidation that comes from the spirit of pride.

FALSE AUTHORITY

False authority is another common trap of Satan. In a word, false authority is witchcraft. "Witchcraft is counterfeit spiritual authority; it is using a spirit other than the Holy Spirit to dominate, manipulate, or control others."[34]

It would seem to be easy to detect something as dark and evil as witchcraft, but that is not always the case. Our discernment can falter in the face of what Lester Sumrall identified as the seven-stage development of demonic influence: regression, repression, suppression, depression, oppression, obsession, and possession.[35] Like the people of Thyatira,[36] we tolerate manipulative leaders who operate in the spirit of Jezebel and her husband, Ahab.[37] Then we lose hope and fall into depression and oppression, which further clouds our discernment and which renders us ineffective in combating evil. The controlling spirit stings us repeatedly, weakening us and causing us to retreat in

---

34. Joyner, *Overcoming Evil*, 75.
35. See, for example, Lester Sumrall, *Exorcism* (Green Forest AR: Green Leaf Press, 1994), 173–192.
36. *"To the angel of the church in Thyatira write:…'I know your deeds, your love and faith, your service and perseverance, and that you are now doing more than you did at first. Nevertheless, I have this against you: You tolerate that woman Jezebel, who calls herself a prophet. By her teaching she misleads my servants into sexual immorality and the eating of food sacrificed to idols'"* (Revelation 2:18–20).
37. *"Surely there was no one like Ahab who sold himself to do evil in the sight of the LORD, because Jezebel his wife incited him"* (1 Kings 21:25 NASB).

discouragement, confusion, disorientation, loss of vision, despair, and defeat.

We may flee from our church or another scene of the wrongful domination, but sadly, that often doesn't alleviate our pain. Lonely and bitter, we say we cannot trust authority figures anymore because of what so-and-so did. Or we remain physically present, maintaining a passive "never open your mouth" policy. Or we become agitators. Still hounded by the unrighteous domination, we lose discernment and do not know what to do about it.

I can guarantee you that the spirit of witchcraft is not going to apologize for making our life so unpleasant. When I find myself in this kind of situation, I need to be careful about taking offense (a topic I will cover in more detail in the next section) or starting to align myself with the accuser of the brethren. The only way to get free of the oppression is to totally forgive those involved—not hanging on to any resentment—to bless all enemies, and to choose to worship God in the midst of the mess.

Yes, I may need to change to a new church. But I will not recover my footing if I go off on my own, saying, "It's just me and Jesus." I need the body of Christ, even with its risks of spiritual and emotional hazards, and the body of Christ needs me and my family.

Moreover, I can't make everything right on my own, because the battle between true and false authority is too big for me. Ultimately, God will prevail. Once again, I must purposefully ally myself with Him and let Him challenge the evil forces: *Be wise in what is good, and simple concerning evil. And the God of peace will crush Satan under your feet shortly*" (Romans 16:19–20 NKJV).

THE SPIRIT OF OFFENSE

The Greek word for "offend" comes from the word *skandalon*, which originally referred to the trigger of a trap, to which the bait was attached. Logically, anything that offends us is in fact a trap that we must watch out for. Offenses pile up and become quarrels, and we almost always do not notice the trap early enough to avoid it, although we can learn to discern more clearly in order to walk more carefully.

As my friend John Bevere pointed out in his book *The Bait of Satan*, "One of his most deceptive and insidious kinds of bait is something every Christian has encountered—offense. Actually, offense itself is not deadly—if it stays in the trap. But if we pick it up and consume it and feed on it in our hearts, then we have become offended."[38] Let's not take the bait!

People who are quarrelsome or adversarial have tripped the trap and become ensnared. What's worse, as the offenses control them and their behavior toward others, they may not recognize the fact that they are being held prisoner to do the devil's will. Jesus said, "*It is inevitable that stumbling blocks come, but woe to him through whom they come!*" (Luke 17:1 NASB). Paul advised:

> *A servant of the Lord must not quarrel but be gentle to all, able to teach, patient, in humility correcting those who are in opposition, if God perhaps will grant them repentance, so that they may know the truth, and that they may come to their senses and escape the snare of the devil, having been taken captive by him to do his will.*
>
> (2 Timothy 2:24–26 NKJV)

Offended people fall into two major categories: (1) those who have been treated unjustly, and (2) those who believe with all their hearts that they have been wronged, judging by "assumption, appearance, and hearsay."[39] Either way, the only effective escape from the trap is not more agitation or argument but, again, forgiveness, total forgiveness.

This is why I pray the Lord's Prayer almost every day, and when I come to the line, "Forgive us our trespasses as we forgive those who trespass against us," I think about my current relationships. Even if I was 90 percent right in an argument with someone, what about that 10 percent where I was wrong? Even if my words were accurate, could I have somehow responded differently so that the other party would

---

38. John Bevere, *The Bait of Satan* (Lake Mary, FL: Charisma House, 1994, 2014), 1.
39. This material was inspired by *The Bait of Satan*, 6–7.

have perceived my response as being given in love instead of harsh judgment or correction?

This approach helps me to sort through my reactions to everything from major power struggles to irritating Facebook posts. Forgiveness works wonders to straighten me out. Then I can overcome the enemy, hear God's voice clearly again, and walk in the fullness of His will. And then Romans 8:28 comes into play, which says, *"And we know that God causes all things to work together for good to those who love God, to those who are called according to His purpose"* (NASB).

John Bevere and his wife, Lisa, came out as overcomers in a situation of serious offense. They successfully moved away physically from the polluting influences that could have destroyed their marriage and ministry, but most important, they forgave all offenders completely. They learned that walking in forgiveness deprives the enemy of "landing strips" in our soul. They discovered that they could rise above any amount of betrayal and shoddy treatment. Forgiveness, humiliating and even weak as it can seem, is a potent antidote to the demonic toxins that would otherwise bring us down to the enemy's level.

THE ENEMY'S PLAN VERSUS GOD'S PLAN

Satan's objective is to rob the Son of God of His place with the Father and the honor that is due Him from the people of earth. His goal is to gain as much control as possible of the world system, so that he can receive universal worship for himself. It was that way with Lucifer in the very beginning, and his goal and tactics remain the same today.

When we look around us and evaluate our personal struggles in this light, we can see why the spiritual warfare rages on and on. Behind the scenes, it is all about Jesus's placement, because all true spiritual warfare ultimately centers on the prominence of the Son of God. We should ask ourselves: Is Jesus the central focus of my heart and life? Do I see attempts by evil forces to push Jesus aside? Is He the Lord over this person or group or place—or has His lordship been undermined and usurped by Satan? Have we as the people of God fallen into the traps that the enemy keeps setting? How can we discern the way ahead and maintain a clear focus?

God's objective is to reap the earth's last great harvest of souls and to prepare the bride of Christ as a gift for His Son. Christ has given us as His disciples the authority to enforce the victory of Calvary. This includes restraining Satan's demonic activities on earth until God's purposes and plans of grace have been fulfilled (see Matthew 16:19; 18:18), and displacing the works of darkness by demonstrating the works of Christ (see, for example, Matthew 10:1, 7–8).

> ALL TRUE SPIRITUAL WARFARE
> ULTIMATELY CENTERS ON THE
> PROMINENCE OF THE SON OF GOD.

We can fulfill these responsibilities because, at the end of His life on earth, Jesus transferred His authority to His followers. He commissioned them, saying,

> *All authority in heaven and on earth has been given to me. Therefore go and make disciples of all nations, baptizing them in the name of the Father and of the Son and of the Holy Spirit, and teaching them to obey everything I have commanded you. And surely I am with you always, to the very end of the age.*
> (Matthew 28:18–20)

Because Jesus paid the ransom for our souls (see, for example, Romans 5:8; 6:23; Galatians 3:13–14), we now go forth as His ambassadors (see, for example, Matthew 28:19–20), carrying the revelation that He who is in us is greater than he who is in the world (see 1 John 4:4; Ephesians 1:17–22; 4:8–9). We gladly submit to God with humility, and even our submission is a form of spiritual warfare: *"Therefore submit to God. Resist the devil and he will flee from you"* (James 4:7 NKJV).

My youngest daughter had an experience that illustrates this point well. When she was eighteen, she received a partial scholarship to attend the New York Conservatory of Dramatic Arts in New York City. Eventually, in one of her classes, she was presented with a script that contained a lot of foul language. She wasn't sure she should perform it; she felt it would compromise her integrity and cause her to step away from the purity of her walk with Christ. She consulted me about it, and I didn't feel good about it, either. But I didn't forbid her from doing the assignment. She was a young adult, and I knew she needed to make up her own mind what to do. I told her something like this: "If you move your boundary once, it will be a lot easier to move it again. So you need to walk wisely if you're thinking of moving your boundary the first time."

Then, interestingly, God gave a dream to one of her brothers who had been very close to her growing up, and he warned her on the phone not to make an unwise decision that would compromise her walk with the Lord. With both my caution and his warning to back her up, she went to her professor and told him that, although she was quite willing to act the part, she was not willing to use the language in the script, that it would violate her conscience to do so. She spoke up even though she risked getting a bad grade or being reprimanded or ostracized.

Amazingly, the instructor listened to her and respected her stance. In fact, he opened the next class by bringing Rachel's appeal before everyone. He said, "Rachel has told me that it would offend her conscience to cuss in this script. Is there anybody else here that feels the same way and who really wishes not to follow the script?" Several others raised their hands. He allowed those students to substitute alternate terminology, and the problem was solved.

Rachel had avoided one of the enemy's traps. She did not start to move her boundaries of righteousness. And she was actually respected for it. She remained submitted to God. She resisted the devil. And he fled.

REACHING FOR A HIGHER REALM

Humility, walking in the nature of Christ, is our goal. Only in going lower will we be able to reach the higher realms of God's kingdom. With humble hearts, we can admit that we have mixed motives and that we have fallen for the enemy's deceptions more than once. Our masquerades and disguises may fool the people around us for a while, but they are useless before God, who already knows us through and through. We cannot hide from Him, so we might as well surrender to Him. After all, He loves us better than we love ourselves. He will sort out the most tangled situations. He always sees the end from the beginning.

It is a fact: God uses only *broken* men and women. People who are self-confident will soon reach the end of their strength. The only way to mount up with the wings of eagles (see Isaiah 40:31) is to surrender everything to God, who is our Strength, our Song (see Exodus 15:2 NASB, NKJV, KJV), and our Father. He does not want us to disqualify ourselves from His kingdom, so He will help us uncover the fingerprints of Satan on places in our hearts that we did not know he could touch.

PRAYER OF A DISCERNING HEART

My Father in heaven, may Your name be hallowed wherever I go as Your ambassador. I ask for wisdom beyond my years so that I can avoid the pitfalls of the enemy. Thank You for exposing his evil plots to my growing discernment. I lay down my masks and rest in Your presence. Search my heart and expose every hidden agenda to Your brilliant light. I give You permission to convict me of any way in which I have compromised with Satan. I surrender my past, present, and future into Your hands, Lord, and I pray for a higher degree of discernment as I walk through my days and nights. Help me to exercise Your kingdom authority and to dislodge any hindrances that block the way ahead. I praise Your name, Jesus, and I thank You. Amen.

11

CREATING A SAFE PLACE: CULTIVATING A CULTURE OF WISDOM AND FAITH

*"Therefore everyone who hears these words of Mine
and acts on them, may be compared to a wise man who
built his house on the rock."*
—Matthew 7:24 (NASB)

As we discern our way through the issues that confront us daily, at times it may feel like we are walking through a maze, frequently bumping into walls and dead ends. I know what that feels like; I have bumped my head against many walls in my own personal discernment development. Yet that is how the learning process works. Even so, we are not alone in this process. We can be part of a community of believers that helps us move safely through the maze and into the light of truth and discernment.

I started learning about mazes early in life. Let me tell you a rather bizarre story about my youthful inquisitiveness that I have never publicly told before but illustrates the possibilities and challenges of creating a culture of wisdom and faith as a spiritual "safe place."

LESSONS FROM MY YOUTH

In high school, I loved biology, and I participated in many different science experiments. My imagination was captured by the adventures of Jacques Cousteau, and I became excited about the idea of building safe housing within the ocean where human beings could live comfortably. I believed the ocean was the last frontier available to support an exploding world population. So at the age of sixteen, for my entry into the high school science fair, I attempted to develop a prototype—a sealed, waterproof glass house where my pet hamster could live for an extended period of time surrounded by the water and fish of my aquarium.

It took me weeks to build this safe place. After exhausting the resources at the school library, I wrote to the state capital library for books on futuristic views and survivalism. My dad helped me cut the glass for my creation, and I investigated every form of waterproof glue that existed. I even figured out a way to pump in air through a tube, and of course I arranged for water and food supply.

To get my hamster, Henry, into the underwater house, I devised a complex maze to run him through, with the reward of food at the end. This preliminary test would last for twenty-one days before the grand immersion. Once he mastered the maze and reached his unique house under the water, I was going to test the effects of long-term underwater living. I just knew I was about to achieve a significant breakthrough! Some people might think I was one weird kid, but I considered myself the farsighted developer of safe housing for the generations to come.

However, things didn't turn out the way I had planned.

Henry completed the twenty-one days working his way through my head-knocking maze and found himself in his new, experimental safe house under the water. He did not like it. Apparently, I had not factored in a few details, like dealing with hamster droppings. Some other minor issues came up, such as how to keep the air moving in and out. I think it was around day three of my proposed seven days that I decided I would have to rescue Henry from his unsafe house. I took him out of the glass container, and I was going to run him through the maze again, but he decided he no longer wanted to participate in my rat race. I imagine him thinking, *Twenty-one more days in a maze? Oh, forget it!* Showing signs of bewilderment, Henry just dropped over and gave up the ghost!

So much for winning first place in the science fair! My career of mastering the final frontier of underwater living was officially over.

CREATING A TRUE SAFE PLACE

Strange illustration, right? But perhaps this youthful experiment served me well in the years to come. It seared into me a desire to search for the wisdom by which a true safe house could be built. My concern became much broader—the building of a safe house for the body of Christ, a place that not only could protect us from death-dealing assaults from the enemy, but where even our imperfect starts and failures could be transformed, a place that celebrated the faith to rise up and try again.

> I STILL BELIEVE IN THIS PALATIAL PLACE CALLED THE CHURCH WHERE LOVE HAS THE FINAL SAY, A PLACE THAT CELEBRATES THE FAITH TO RISE UP AND TRY AGAIN.

I guess I have remained a dreamer to this day. I dream of the body of Christ being a place where births may be messy, but where newborn babes can learn to crawl, stand, and walk; a place where adolescents can learn from their mistakes and the members of the community can rally together to cheer each other on.

Yes, I still believe in this palatial place called the church where love has the final say; and over the years, I have discovered a few commodities necessary for constructing a spiritual safe place. Foundational elements appear to include the following: (1) authentic faith, (2) godly core values, (3) walking in Christ's authority, (4) walking in community, and (5) powerful proclamations. To incorporate each of these components, we must receive—and give—wisdom from above that is beyond our years. (See James 3:17 NASB, NKJV, KJV.)

1. AUTHENTIC FAITH

LOOKING TO JESUS, ABIDING WITH GOD

How do we develop authentic faith? When we "[fix] *our eyes on Jesus, the pioneer and perfecter of faith*" (Hebrews 12:2), our faith grows truer and stronger. Even our worst failures turn into victories when faith gets a firm grip on them.

Faith gives us our connection with God. As we have been learning throughout this book, our ability to discern the difference between good and evil depends on the health of that connection. From time to time, often without meaning to, we wander away from God because we are lured by enticing messages that are contrary to His Word, His will, and His ways. We do not realize at first that these words originate from the enemy of our souls, Satan, because they sound so convincing or alluring. Somehow we forget essential elements of our belief—such as the facts that God is good and He loves us. But when we step outside boundaries we used to respect, we also step outside God's safe pasture.

I have gleaned extraordinary wisdom from the ministry of Bill Johnson of Bethel Church in Redding, California. In his book *God Is Good*, Bill aptly states, "Believing that God is good is absolutely vital to becoming effective in the ministry of the Gospel. Our endurance in representing Jesus well and consistently is dependent on this one thing. God is absolute goodness."[40]

When we lose sight of such essential elements of our belief, our faith flaps in the breeze like loose tackle on a sailboat, and we do not know how to readily secure it again. This scenario does not have to happen as often as it does—if we have true safe places where the faith and discernment of others can shore up our own faith and discernment when they are weak. If we live in the context of a healthy community

---

40. Bill Johnson, *God Is Good* (Shippensburg, PA: Destiny Image, 2016), 164.

within the body of Christ, we can get reoriented quickly. We can also take what we have learned and use it to help others in the same way we have been helped.

I'm talking about more than having a place where people can give you good advice, although good advice should be available in a safe place. Rather, a safe place is characterized by mutual protectiveness—people looking out for each other and caring about each other deeply. Believers create a safe-place culture when, together, they live out the reality of the kingdom of God: They point each other to the Lord and remind each other of how faith works. They take shelter from the spiritual wilderness of the world at large. They share insights and real-life struggles. They pray and proclaim truth that comes straight from the Word of God. And, instead of running away at the first sign of interpersonal tension (taking cues from the "divorce culture" of the world around them), they stick together, forgive, and work things out. There is not one rock star or lone ranger among them.

Does this sound like something foreign to you? Or have you been blessed in your church or family with such a safe place? It is my conviction that we cannot flourish and grow as part of the body of Christ without such a place. When we try to live for God on our own, we are like foolish lambs who graze at the edge of the flock, becoming easy prey to the enemy—the lion who prowls around *"seeking someone to devour"* (1 Peter 5:8 NASB). The voice of the Shepherd is harder to discern the farther away you wander from the safe pasture.

Creating a culture of faith is both a goal and a lifestyle. Above, I quoted Bill Johnson of Bethel Church. In a very intentional way, Bethel Church and hundreds of other churches are nurturing an alternative culture of faith and mutual honor that is also energized by a high level of expectation for hearing the voice of God. It is contagious.

Since God is the ultimate Safe Place for every one of us, and since His Spirit dwells within us both individually and corporately, we truly need each other in the church. Let us build authentic faith together, beginning by affirming our reliance on the God who allows us to dwell in the *"secret place of the Most High"*:

He who dwells in the secret place of the Most High shall abide under the shadow of the Almighty. I will say of the LORD, "He is my refuge and my fortress; my God, in Him I will trust."

(Psalm 91:1–2 NKJV)

> WHEN WE LOSE SIGHT OF ESSENTIAL ELEMENTS OF OUR BELIEF, OUR FAITH FLAPS IN THE BREEZE LIKE LOOSE TACKLE ON A SAILBOAT.

COUNTERACT FEAR

Another way to cultivate authentic faith is to replace our fear with trust in God's power and provision. Jesus warned that in the difficult times to come, many people's hearts would fail due to fear. (See Luke 21:26.) Fear is the opposite of faith. Therefore, cultivating faith is the only way to counter the fear that arises within us in times of trouble. That faith, however, must be firmly rooted and grounded in Jesus's victory on the cross. Such faith cannot be learned by rote memorization of facts, inherited from a parent, or purchased on the Internet. Faith is a living thing, and it must be nurtured daily.

Alongside other believers, we can work to create a culture of faith in the midst of a very real culture of fear. The powers of evil remain active throughout the earth at all times, whether or not their strategies can be discerned by the average person. The prevalence of fear in the world should prove that demonic wickedness is not dead. People suffer from the darkness even though the crucified Jesus put Satan under His feet once and for all when He rose from the dead. Those outside the body of Christ cannot find the security of a safe place, even though they make every effort to do so. It does not occur to them that the church holds what they seek. They just do not know the whole story.

On the cross, when Jesus gasped, *"It is finished"* (John 19:30) and subsequently sent His Spirit to dwell in the hearts of His followers, He was creating for us not only the best safe place but the only true one. To this day, He is still saying to faithful believers what He said through the prophet Haggai: *"My Spirit is abiding in your midst; do not fear!"* (Haggai 2:5 NASB). We must realize that it is our faith, shared with others, that enforces the victory of Calvary. Together, we work and pray for God's kingdom to come on earth as it is in heaven. We learn to discern His hand in human affairs and to collaborate with Him in supplanting Satan.

One glorious day, Jesus will return to fully establish His kingdom rule on earth. What you believe about that significantly influences your faith; accordingly, it determines the way you live, as we will explore in the next section.

2. GODLY CORE VALUES

CORE VALUES CREATE LIFESTYLE

The Lord spoke to me about my core values more than forty years ago when I was a young pastor, and what I learned then has stuck with me. At the time, I was not thinking forty or fifty or a hundred years into the future; I was just thinking about the week ahead and my next Sunday sermon. Yet out of the blue, this sentence occurred to me, and I knew it was from God: *Your end-time worldview will determine your lifestyle.*

The Lord wasn't delineating to me what my end-time worldview should be. He was simply pointing out that my day-to-day decisions, taken together, would create my style of life. Inevitably, these decisions would be based on my faith. How would my core values be affected by what I thought about Christ's return? How would I interpret the Scriptures? Would I view myself as helping to bring God's kingdom to earth? What might be my contribution to this purpose? What kind of education would I acquire in relation to it?

Over time, my worldview and my approach to everything in life has turned out to align with these four core biblical values:

1. God is good, all the time.

2. Nothing is impossible with God.

3. Everything that needed to be accomplished was completed at Calvary.

4. As ambassadors of Christ, we carry His delegated, regal authority.

Again, forty years have gone by since the Lord first spoke to me about core values, and as it has turned out, I have given my life to raising up a people who are so filled with the Holy Spirit that His light shining through them can replace the darkness. I have endeavored to understand God's kingdom and, like the sons of Issachar, to discern the times and the seasons in order to teach people how to live wisely. (See 1 Chronicles 12:32.) I may not have succeeded in every respect, but I aim to finish as well as I can. I want to live in and share an authentic culture of wisdom and faith until the day God calls me home.

CORE VALUES SHAPE ATTITUDES AND EXPECTATIONS

Our enemy would like to deflect us from the purposes of God by inserting ungodly beliefs into our minds, but the Spirit helps us to uncover those negative strongholds, and with His help we can replace them with positive attitudes and applications.[41] For example, when I discover that I am being plagued by the fear that God has passed me by, giving good things to other people but not to me, I call up the truth that God is good, all the time. I allow my biblical core values to shape my attitudes and expectations. Otherwise, I will view my memories of past experiences, my present tribulations, and my uncertain future through a dark lens, and my faith will falter.

I lay hold of this truth: we do not fight *toward* victory—we fight *from* victory. Jesus has already won the battle. He has overcome the world. Thus, when evil washes over me and I am tempted to despair,

---

41. Again, the biblical support for this comes from 2 Corinthians 10:5: "*We demolish arguments and every pretension that sets itself up against the knowledge of God, and we take captive every thought to make it obedient to Christ.*"

I can discern the desperate efforts of the devil to persuade me that Jesus's victory is not true.

I also learn to embrace the humbling circumstances in which I find myself. I have adopted a new attitude about humility. The world tells me that I should be powerful, capable, strong, respected—while keeping up a front of false modesty so nobody will criticize me. But Jesus tells me that true humility paves the way to His kind of success. I have discovered through experience that false humility will deny my true destiny, while true humility will take me to it. Our boasting should be in what Christ has already accomplished, not in our human ability to bring His earthly rule and reign to pass.

The only way you and I can do any good on this earth and help bring in God's kingdom is to let His light shine through our broken, humble selves. When we read a messianic prophecy such as this one from Isaiah, we can discern the mature outworking of God's plan:

> *The Spirit of the Sovereign* LORD *is on me, because the* LORD *has anointed me to proclaim good news to the poor. He has sent me to bind up the brokenhearted, to proclaim freedom for the captives and release from darkness for the prisoners, to proclaim the year of the* LORD's *favor and the day of vengeance of our God, to comfort all who mourn, and provide for those who grieve in Zion—to bestow on them a crown of beauty instead of ashes, the oil of joy instead of mourning, and a garment of praise instead of a spirit of despair. They will be called oaks of righteousness, a planting of the* LORD *for the display of his splendor.* (Isaiah 61:1–3)

Jesus the Messiah is the Light of the World. We are not supposed to merely gaze on Him and reflect His glory; rather, His glory is supposed to burst out of us. We do not deny the darkness, but we do deny its finality. As Isaiah 60:1 encourages, we arise and let His light shine through us. "*To them* [the Lord's people] *God has chosen to make known among the Gentiles the glorious riches of this mystery, which is Christ in you, the hope of glory*" (Colossians 1:27).

Let us endeavor to create a healthy kingdom culture where all believers can shine their light together and thus overwhelm the kingdom of darkness, including every religious and political spirit, every spirit of pride, the antichrist spirit, and anything else that the enemy decides to throw in our faces.

> LET US ENDEAVOR TO CREATE A HEALTHY KINGDOM CULTURE WHERE ALL BELIEVERS CAN SHINE THEIR LIGHT TOGETHER AND THUS OVERWHELM THE KINGDOM OF DARKNESS.

3. WALKING IN THE AUTHORITY OF CHRIST

Walking in the authority of Christ is another important ingredient of a spiritual safe place. When God created Adam and Eve, He told them to have dominion over and subdue all things on earth. (See Genesis 1:26, 28 NKJV, KJV.) In other words, He gave them the authority to act as His stewards. This was not the same as being given *ownership* over all things on earth. God still owned everything, and He still does. "*The earth is the LORD's, and all it contains, the world, and those who dwell in it*" (Psalm 24:1 NASB).

Yet, as we know, Adam and Eve chose to disobey God's clear command, and their disobedience caused a serious separation between them and God. (See Genesis 2:17; 3:6–11, 22–23.) Worse than that, their decision constituted *willful obedience to Satan*. Now they were his slaves, and so were their descendants.[42] Thus, the authority that God had given them was handed over to the enemy.

Not the ownership, remember, just the authority. That's why Satan used this terminology when he tempted Jesus in the wilderness:

---

42. "*Do you not know that to whom you present yourselves slaves to obey, you are that one's slaves whom you obey, whether of sin leading to death, or of obedience leading to righteousness?*" (Romans 6:16 NASB).

"I will give you all [the] *authority and splendor* [of the kingdoms of the world]; *it has been given to me, and I can give it to anyone I want to"* (Luke 4:6). Satan is the *"prince of the power of the air"* (Ephesians 2:2 NASB, NKJV, KJV), and he was given the temporary right to act in the earth's atmosphere.

The authority, however, was transferred back to Jesus when He paid the ransom price for sinful mankind, the life of one sinless Man for all sinners. With His own life, He bought back the authority. That's why Jesus said to His disciples, right before His ascension to heaven, *"All authority in heaven and on earth has been given to me"* (Matthew 28:18). Jesus triumphed over Satan, disarmed the powers of evil, and regained the authority that had been handed over to the darkness by Adam's sin. Jesus is the Lord of all!

> *The Son is the image of the invisible God, the firstborn over all creation. For in him all things were created: things in heaven and on earth, visible and invisible, whether thrones or powers or rulers or authorities; all things have been created through him and for him. He is before all things, and in him all things hold together. And he is the head of the body, the church; he is the beginning and the firstborn from among the dead, so that in everything he might have the supremacy. For God was pleased to have all his fullness dwell in him, and through him to reconcile to himself all things, whether things on earth or things in heaven, by making peace through his blood, shed on the cross.* (Colossians 1:15–20)

What did Jesus do with the authority He recovered? Almost immediately, He gave it back to mankind again—to His followers, to those in whom His Spirit would dwell. (See, for example, John 20:20–22; Acts 1:8; Luke 24:47.) This is the spiritual reality we live in, and our discernment and decisions should increasingly align with it. Paul prayed this prayer for the Ephesian believers, and we can pray it for ourselves so that we might better understand this spiritual reality:

> *I pray that the eyes of your heart may be enlightened, so that you will know what is the hope of His calling, what are the riches of the*

glory of His inheritance in the saints, and what is the surpassing greatness of His power toward us who believe. These are in accordance with the working of the strength of His might which He brought about in Christ, when He raised Him from the dead and seated Him at His right hand in the heavenly places, far above all rule and authority and power and dominion, and every name that is named, not only in this age but also in the one to come. And He put all things in subjection under His feet, and gave Him as head over all things to the church, which is His body, the fullness of Him who fills all in all. (Ephesians 1:18–23 NASB)

Armed with the authority that comes from Jesus's name, we are now to go forth into the world to make disciples. (See Jesus's Great Commission in Matthew 28:19–20.) Everywhere we go, Jesus's Spirit goes, too. And greater is He who is in us than he who is in the world! (See 1 John 4:4.)

Remember, when we walk in the authority of the Word of God, we walk in safety. We need to attain a solid grasp of scriptural principles so that we can discern and decide wisely, as well as help to create and maintain the culture of wisdom and faith that is so important.

4. WALKING IN COMMUNITY

We have already begun to see how walking in community with other believers is an essential aspect of a spiritual safe place as we grow together and continue Jesus's ministry on earth. The body of Christ is God's "building," still a work in progress but useful to Him:

For we are co-workers in God's service; you are God's field, God's building. By the grace God has given me, I laid a foundation as a wise builder, and someone else is building on it. But each one should build with care. (1 Corinthians 3:9–10)

We are being *"built together"* as a habitation for God's Spirit: *"And in him you too are being built together to become a dwelling in which God lives by his Spirit"* (Ephesians 2:22). And that means that we are being built together as people of faith who operate within a culture of faith:

> *Therefore as you have received Christ Jesus the Lord, so walk in Him, having been firmly rooted and now being built up in Him and established in your faith, just as you were instructed, and over-flowing with gratitude.* (Colossians 2:6–7 NASB)

Together, as the body of Christ, we have been authorized to do the works of Jesus in the world today, including signs and wonders and casting out demons. (See Mark 16:17, James 4:7, and many other New Testament passages.) No evil power can overpower us—when we live together in love and faith. (See Ecclesiastes 4:12.)

I think again of the prophet Daniel, who was captured by the Babylonians when he was a young man and exiled to the courts of King Nebuchadnezzar and succeeding kings for the rest of his long life. Daniel was in exile, but he was not alone; he had his three friends, Shadrach, Meshach, and Abednego, with him. Together, they created a culture of wisdom and faith that withstood many intimidations, including death threats. Together, they took shelter under the protective wings of God. The biblical account of their courageous acts provides a graphic glimpse of what a corporate safe place looks like. (See the book of Daniel.) Walking in community, they illustrated the truth of this verse: *"This is the victory that has overcome the world—our faith"* (1 John 5:4 NASB).

> NO EVIL POWER CAN
> OVERPOWER US—WHEN WE
> LIVE TOGETHER IN LOVE AND FAITH.

5. POWERFUL PROCLAMATIONS

Let us look at one other essential component of a culture of wisdom and faith: the power of proclamation. From prayerful proclamation to prophetic proclamation, our faith culture expands and grows deeper roots as God's truth is announced to listening ears. Most fundamentally, we proclaim God's greatness:

> For I proclaim the name of the LORD: ascribe greatness to our God. He is the Rock, His work is perfect; for all His ways are justice, a God of truth and without injustice; righteous and upright is He. (Deuteronomy 32:3–4 NKJV)

Always remember, we are not praying and proclaiming *toward* victory—we are praying and proclaiming *from* a place of victory. There is authentic power in prophetic revelations when we proclaim them within the church community and to the world. As God's people, we know the Lord, and we know our Shepherd's voice. The God who created communication in all its forms is perfectly capable of making Himself understood; He speaks to each of us in ways that we not only can pick up on, but also comprehend. He knows how to speak the language of your soul, and He will give you a song to sing to the world.

You and I, who carry God's Spirit, can proclaim the good news of salvation wherever we go. In a culture of wise faith, after addressing proclamations to God Himself, extolling His greatness, we rise up and declare freedom for the people who walk in darkness—freedom from the spiritual powers of wickedness:

> The Spirit of the Lord GOD is upon me, because the LORD has anointed me to bring good news to the afflicted; He has sent me to bind up the brokenhearted, to proclaim liberty to captives and freedom to prisoners; to proclaim the favorable year of the LORD and the day of vengeance of our God; to comfort all who mourn, to grant those who mourn in Zion, giving them a garland instead of ashes, the oil of gladness instead of mourning, the mantle of praise instead of a spirit of fainting. So they will be called oaks of righteousness, the planting of the LORD, that He may be glorified. (Isaiah 61:1–3 NASB)

Our bold and faith-filled proclamations change the spiritual atmosphere, suffusing it with God's light and presence. We're not people who just bide our time, staying out of trouble and waiting to escape this troubled world. Instead, we bring God's presence right into the world around us, proclaiming His lordship and supremacy and love. We reach out and we intercede. We break bondages and deliver people from captivity.

The whole time, we who dwell in God's safe place rejoice in His greatness, goodness, and love. We can say that we have seen the Lord with our own eyes because we have discerned Him at work in so many places, not the least of which is our own hearts.

REACHING FOR A HIGHER REALM

Come with me—let's reach for the sky! Let's make a binding decision to never, ever give up walking together, with the Lord Jesus Christ and with each other.

> Let the word of Christ richly dwell within you, with all wisdom teaching and admonishing one another with psalms and hymns and spiritual songs, singing with thankfulness in your hearts to God. Whatever you do in word or deed, do all in the name of the Lord Jesus, giving thanks through Him to God the Father.
> (Colossian 3:16–17 NASB)

God is coming *to* us before He's coming *for* us. Come what may, let's be discerners who expect Jesus's return and who prepare for it wisely, leaning on each other and helping each other stay strong in the core values of God's kingdom. Let's build a culture of wisdom and faith, blooming right where He has planted each one of us.

PRAYER OF A DISCERNING HEART

Gracious Father, I choose not to forsake the assembling of believers. I proclaim that we are better together. Together, we have more faith, more power, and more authority. I choose to follow the way of love that creates safe places. I proclaim that I have more faith in Your ability to keep me than I have fear of the enemy's ability to deceive me. In the midst of a culture of faith, I renounce the spirit of fear and any past doctrines or associations in my life that may have promoted a culture of paralyzing fear. I rejoice in the cleansing power of the blood of Jesus, and I want to extend to others the good news of salvation.

Father, Your kingdom has no expiration date! Thank You beyond words for calling me to be part of Your family of faith. Thank You beyond words for calling me to be a resident of Your safe house. In Jesus's precious name, amen.

12

REVELATION'S ULTIMATE PURPOSE: THE WORD BECOMES FLESH

"And the Word became flesh and dwelt among us,
and we beheld His glory, the glory as of the only begotten
of the Father, full of grace and truth."
—John 1:14 (NKJV)

O ne of joys in my life is the people I have the honor of working with. One of them is Jeffrey Thompson, executive director of my ministry, God Encounters Ministries. Here he tells about a revelatory experience he had with the Lord that expresses the theme of this chapter:

One day not long ago, I was given the opportunity to preach at the church where I serve part-time on the pastoral staff. After I brought the message at the worship service, I felt really good about it. It seemed to have been inspired both in content and delivery. So I asked the Lord, "Lord, have You called me to preach?"

The Lord responded to me immediately in my spirit, saying, "No, I've called you to incarnate."

He was realigning my priorities, reminding me that the endgame isn't just the preaching or teaching or whatever—the endgame is the relationship with Jesus Christ; and the more completely I walk with Him, the more I incarnate Him. By "incarnate," I mean He takes on flesh in me. I am called to bring His love and wisdom and peace and hope into the room with me so that people can see Him.

That says it well. The subtitle of this book is *Hearing, Confirming, and Acting on Prophetic Revelation*, and that is fitting. But ultimately, *The Discerner* is a book about incarnation. Not only is it about the historical incarnation of God the Son as a Jewish man named Jesus over two thousand years ago, but also about Jesus's incarnation in each of His followers, in you and in me. Each one of us has been called to incarnate Him.

TRANSFORMED BY REVELATION

How does this incarnation occur? First, Jesus enables us to *receive* His revelation and to *discern* His message out of the chaos of many competing voices. Then He enables us to *become* the revelation! We grow in our likeness to the very Word of God. We incarnate the Word.[43]

The walk of faith that begins as a personal relationship with God moves into a revelatory relationship as we learn how He expresses Himself in so many ways. For most of us, this is enough. And it is true that there's no end to what we need to learn about relationship and revelation in our continuing, lifelong adventure with God. But our end goal is to become so fully transformed into His image that we can represent Him while we live on the earth.

It is a holy progression: relationship produces revelation, and together relationship and revelation give rise to incarnation.

Had you ever thought about that before? Let's review the basics: in the Scriptures, Jesus is referred to as the Word—the Word who became flesh and dwelt among us, the Word who is the glorious, only begotten Son of God, full of grace and truth. (See John 1:1, 14.)

---

43. See John 1:14 at the beginning of this chapter.

Somehow, much of the body of Christ and the global prophetic movement has failed to appreciate these fundamental truths. We are not supposed to only receive revelation, but we are also to become living epistles for all to read![44]

The only begotten Son of God still dwells among us; His Spirit lives in each of us who has named Jesus as Lord. He speaks to us, and we can hear Him. With grace, He reveals His truth to us. His revelation takes many forms, and we share it within and beyond the body of Christ.

And that revelation transforms us, doesn't it? Increasingly, we become more like Him in His love. We may feel as though we wobble and fall like babies learning to walk, but we do learn to walk. Eventually our steps become steadier. Relationship has led to revelation, and revelation has led to incarnation.

In a very real way, as you receive, incorporate, and release Jesus's words, you become a living epistle for other people to read. Discerners graft the Word of God into their hearts and souls and minds. Not only can they discern good and evil with increasing skill, but they can also determine what to do with that information. They learn how to cast down every stronghold that exalts itself against the knowledge of God. (See 2 Corinthians 10:5.) They learn what it means to pick up their cross daily and deny themselves (see Luke 9:23) so that they can live out the new reality of "Christ in us, the hope of glory, full of grace and truth" (see Colossians 1:27).

Discerners do not operate by themselves, because they ally with other like-minded followers of Christ. They appreciate the varied gifts that God has given to the members of His body. They can see how God's gifts and graces are working together to make the church, as the bride of Christ, ready for her Bridegroom, Jesus:

Christ loved the church and gave himself up for her to make her holy, cleansing her by the washing with water through the word, and...present[ing] her to himself as a radiant church, without

---

44. You can learn more about incarnational Christianity in my book *The Lost Art of Practicing His Presence* (Shippensburg, PA: Destiny Image, 2006).

stain or wrinkle or any other blemish, but holy and blameless.
                                                    (Ephesians 5:25–27)

Tying everything together is love. (See Colossians 3:14.) I learned from one of my prophetic mentors, seer Bob Jones, to ask the questions, "Did I exhibit love?" "Did I learn to love?" With Christ's love and power and character and mind incarnated in us, the church is unbeatable. The enemy can batter us, but he can't eliminate us. Individually and corporately, we are like the unbreakable three-cord strand of Ecclesiastes' proverb: *"Though one may be overpowered, two can defend themselves. A cord of three strands is not quickly broken"* (Ecclesiastes 4:12). As individuals and as a body, we never stop growing in the fullness of relationship, gifting, fruitfulness, revelation, wisdom, and incarnation.

> WITH CHRIST'S LOVE AND POWER
> AND CHARACTER AND MIND INCARNATED
> IN US, THE CHURCH IS UNBEATABLE.

WALKING IN INCARNATIONAL CHRISTIANITY

PRESENTING JESUS TO THE WORLD

All of this is to say one thing: the whole purpose of prophetic revelation and therefore the purpose of the discerner of revelation is incarnational—presenting Jesus to the world. This is the reason for our interactive hearing and communing with God in all of its dimensions. Together with all of those who walk with Jesus, we carry His message to the world.

As the apostle John was recording the magnificent revelation that he received when he was on the Isle of Patmos, he wrote:

I fell at [the angel's] feet to worship him. But he said to me, "Do not do that; I am a fellow servant of yours and your brethren who hold the testimony of Jesus; worship God. For the testimony of Jesus is the spirit of prophecy." (Revelation 19:10 NASB)

For us as discerners, the key phrase here is *"your brethren who hold the testimony of Jesus."* If our receiving revelation does not lead others into a greater awareness of who Christ Jesus is, and if it does not lead us into a more passionate pursuit of Him, then something is askew. A lot of people have historical information and even doctrinal knowledge about Jesus, but we must have a personal revelation of Him. We cannot find this without the help of His Holy Spirit, because it takes God to know God. One of the Holy Spirit's roles is to make Jesus real to us, to make us able to know Him and follow Him. As we know Him, we make Him known—through our words and our lifestyle. We incarnate Him, carrying His testimony far and wide.

So when we talk about receiving and releasing prophetic revelation, we are not primarily referring to predicting the future, but rather to displaying the message and person of Jesus to the world around us. This is something that you and I can do. With the Holy Spirit helping us, we can "show and tell" the world that Jesus is Lord and Messiah. (See Matthew 16:13–17; 1 Corinthians 12:3.)

True prophetic revelation is powerful; it penetrates hardened hearts and unbelief. Think about how it worked in the New Testament. When Jesus told Nathanael that He had seen him under the fig tree, Nathanael and others believed that Jesus was the Messiah. (See John 1:43–51.) After Jesus revealed to the Samaritan woman at the well "everything she ever did," and she told the people of her town about it, many of the townspeople came to believe in Him as the Son of God. (See John 4:7–26.) This is the revelation lifestyle we are meant to be walking in today. Living a life of revelation can change people's lives. And as you and I walk with Jesus, we step into the same powerful, revelatory stream that He walked in.

REVELATORY ENCOUNTERS WITH JESUS TODAY

A few years ago, I went to Indonesia to minister at a conference with Bill Johnson, Ché Ahn, and Heidi Baker. Indonesia, made up of thousands of islands in Southeast Asia, is the largest Muslim-populated nation in the world. For safety, I was given a personal body-guard who went everywhere with me. He was a dedicated Muslim who had never been in a church meeting in his life. He also had never been taught the truth about Jesus as Savior and Lord, though his religion had taught him to believe that Jesus was one of the prophets.

As I was at the podium speaking in one of the sessions, my body-guard stood nearby. Everything I taught at the conference was being translated into the Indonesian language, so he was able to understand it. And during my message, unbeknownst to me, he had a revelatory encounter with God. I found out about it the next day right before I got up to speak again. People were taking turns sharing testimonies, and I was sitting in the first row with some friends who were translating for me. Much to my surprise, my Muslim bodyguard went up front to testify.

He started off by stating, "Listen to Prophet James Goll." I do not know if anybody told him to call me that, but it did make me think of the Scripture passage that says if you receive a prophet in the name of a prophet, you'll receive a prophet's reward.[45] Then he went on to say, "I am a Muslim, and while I was serving Prophet James Goll I had a vision. Light and glory came, and many angels appeared to me." People applauded. He was finished, so I got up to speak.

While I was giving my message, this man had a second vision, a panoramic one, while his eyes were open and he was just standing there as my bodyguard. This time, Jesus—along with His disciples—appeared to him, and Jesus spoke to him, saying, "Would you be one of My disciples?" On the spot, pierced by the revelation, this man gave his heart to the Lord Jesus Christ.

When I heard about this later, I was amazed. I have never known of anyone having a vision of Jesus with all His disciples. This powerful encounter had long-lasting results. The man was a husband and father, and eventually his whole family gave their lives to Jesus. On a later trip

---

45. *"He who receives a prophet in the name of a prophet shall receive a prophet's reward; and he who receives a righteous man in the name of a righteous man shall receive a righteous man's reward"* (Matthew 10:41 NASB).

REVELATION'S ULTIMATE PURPOSE: THE WORD BECOMES FLESH 189

to Indonesia, I was told that they had all become part of a local church and been water-baptized. This was God moving in signs and wonders, praise the Lord!

When you and I and others carry the Spirit of God into a dark place, the glory of His light sweeps away all obstacles and overcomes the darkness. Amazing things can happen, whether or not you expect them to. Revelatory gifts are like anti-tank missiles. They shatter the enemy's schemes, expose darkness, and release freedom to captives.

> IF OUR RECEIVING REVELATION DOES NOT LEAD OTHERS INTO A GREATER AWARENESS OF WHO CHRIST JESUS IS, AND IF IT DOES NOT LEAD US INTO A MORE PASSIONATE PURSUIT OF HIM, THEN SOMETHING IS ASKEW.

A CULTURE OF HONOR

When my Indonesian bodyguard gave honor to me, he was giving honor to my God, and he was rewarded richly. The Scriptures urge us to cultivate a culture of honor both within the body of Christ and wherever we go. For example, Paul wrote to the church in Rome, *"Be devoted to one another in love. Honor one another above yourselves"* (Romans 12:10).

We cultivate a culture of honor within the church when we hold other believers up, esteeming them for their contributions to God's kingdom. Essentially, we are honoring them for incarnating Christ. No one person can incarnate the Lord Jesus Christ in every regard, of course. But collectively, we can embody Him.

In my own life, I will never run out of people to honor, and I honor each of them for a different reason. I think of everybody from my own praying mother to apostolic teacher and church growth expert C. Peter

Wagner, who graduated to glory even as I was working on this book. I think of Ché Ahn and Don Finto, wonderful apostolic leaders who have walked with me through good times and bad. You can look at my recommended reading list at the end of this book for some of the many people I honor by name. I would add to that list many nameless ones who may not have published books but who have incarnated Christ's love for me. These are some of the true believers who have incarnated the compassion and virtues of the Lord Jesus Christ. I honor them all. I am a man most grateful.

ACTING IN THE OPPOSITE SPIRIT

By cultivating a culture of honor, we actually engage in a form of spiritual warfare. The enemy cannot block our way when we act in a manner that is opposite to his spirit of confusion, pride, control, and destruction. Quite simply, we overcome evil with good. As Paul put it:

> *Let love be without hypocrisy. Abhor what is evil; cling to what is good. Be devoted to one another in brotherly love; give preference to one another in honor; not lagging behind in diligence, fervent in spirit, serving the Lord; rejoicing in hope, persevering in tribulation, devoted to prayer, contributing to the needs of the saints, practicing hospitality. Bless those who persecute you; bless and do not curse. Rejoice with those who rejoice, and weep with those who weep. Be of the same mind toward one another; do not be haughty in mind, but associate with the lowly. Do not be wise in your own estimation. Never pay back evil for evil to anyone. Respect what is right in the sight of all men. If possible, so far as it depends on you, be at peace with all men. Never take your own revenge, beloved, but leave room for the wrath of God, for it is written, "Vengeance is Mine, I will repay," says the Lord. "But if your enemy is hungry, feed him, and if he is thirsty, give him a drink; for in so doing you will heap burning coals on his head." Do not be overcome by evil, but overcome evil with good.* (Romans 12:9–21 NASB)

As incarnational Christians, discerners embody the Word. They discern good and evil and receive revelation, interpretation, and appropriate application. They purposefully make godly distinctions and act on them wisely and lovingly. This enables them to square off against evil by walking in the nature of Christ.

Acting in the opposite spirit, as taught by Jesus in the Sermon on the Mount (see Matthew 5–7) is one of the best ways to combat the religious spirit or any other pervasive spirit. Thus, judgment is overcome by blessing, and criticism by redemptive evaluation. Legalism is dismantled by grace. Competitive debate is dissipated by wise and uplifting speech. Deception is penetrated by truth.

At this point in time, every act of spiritual warfare is leading up to an end-time battle. It behooves each one of us to become discerners who, like the ancient priests of Zadok (see Ezekiel 44:15–23), not only can tell the difference between the holy and the profane, but can instruct others as well. We need to learn to live by the words of Jesus and also teach them to others. Most often, our actions speak louder than our words.

Relationship. Revelation. Incarnation. This is our aim; this is our goal! When we receive, discern, and communicate revelation from God, we become a word from Him that penetrates the darkness by turning on the light.

REACHING FOR A HIGHER REALM

I have been talking about *"Christ in you, the hope of glory"* (Colossians 1:27). As people who embody Christ Jesus, we embody hope—and hope is a *Person.* Even in the darkest places, we let His light shine in. We are ambassadors for the kingdom of God, and together we represent our King in the world. *"Therefore, we are ambassadors for Christ, as though God were making an appeal through us; we beg you on behalf of Christ, be reconciled to God"* (2 Corinthians 5:20 NASB).

I was once ministering at Bishop Joseph Garlington's Covenant Church in Pittsburgh, Pennsylvania, when right in the middle of my sermon the Holy Spirit asked me a question. In my heart, I heard, *How do you cast a shadow?* It did not really make any sense to me at that moment. I kept on preaching, but inside I was multitasking as I mulled over the question.

After I finished speaking, I called about a dozen people up for ministry. I was trying to discern what to pray for them when I remembered that little question, and it made me start singing the old popular song "Me and My Shadow." As I moved, I noticed that the platform lights were casting a noticeable shadow of myself across the floor, so I started to prophetically dramatize the words. When I got to the phrase "strolling down the avenue," I moved along the row of people, with my shadow falling on each one of them in turn—and they were overwhelmed with the power of the Holy Spirit. Ha! He had done it again! His presence had come and overshadowed these believers with His love and care.

Later, the Holy Spirit shared a secret with me that answered His question, "How do you cast a shadow?" The people who cast a shadow are those who "walk in the light." After I received that word, I began to ask people, "Is your shadow dangerous? Does it confront the powers of darkness?" Indeed, followers of Christ cast a shadow by standing in His light, and the closer to the light we get, the longer and stronger the shadow will be. Remember what happened with Peter's shadow in the early church?

> *Believers were increasingly added to the Lord, multitudes of both men and women, so that they brought the sick out into the streets and laid them on beds and couches, that at least the shadow of Peter passing by might fall on some of them.*
>
> (Acts 5:14–15 NKJV)

Wouldn't you like to see things like that happen in your own life? Step closer and closer to Jesus. Lean on His breast as John did. (See John 13:23.) Listen for His heartbeat. Let your heart beat in rhythm with His heart; let your hearts beat as one. See what happens.

As we close this final chapter of *The Discerner*, which I trust has been instructional, inspirational, and revelatory for you, I want make sure that you know one essential principle: These truths are not for an elite group of upper-class Christians. No! What I have shared with you from the depths of my heart is meant for every believer. The only requirement is hunger. Are you hungry for more of the Lord? You can count on the truth of this saying: "The depth of your hunger is the length of your reach to God."

I don't know about you, but I want to do more than hear a word from God. I want to *become* that word. That is revelation's ultimate purpose—for the Word to become flesh.

> RELATIONSHIP. REVELATION. INCARNATION. THIS IS OUR AIM; THIS IS OUR GOAL! WHEN WE RECEIVE, DISCERN, AND COMMUNICATE REVELATION FROM GOD, WE BECOME A WORD FROM HIM THAT PENETRATES THE DARKNESS BY TURNING ON THE LIGHT.

PRAYER OF A DISCERNING HEART

Our Father, in Jesus's name and as a New Testament believer, I want to become part of the living Word of God. Along with others in the body of Christ, I want to become more mature and to surrender my senses to the Holy Spirit. By grace, I want to grow in my discernment of good and evil. I want to grow in my ability to receive Your revelation and to release it to others as You guide me. I want to carry the fragrance of heaven wherever I go and to touch others with Your love. Faithfully, I want to cultivate a culture of honor and to become an ambassador of hope. My greatest hope is to continue with the company of Jesus's disciples who embody the Word of God until I draw my final breath on earth. With a joyful amen!

RECOMMENDED READING

Baker, Heidi. *Compelled by Love*. Lake Mary, FL: Charisma House, 2008.

Bevere, John. *The Bait of Satan*, 20th ann. ed. Lake Mary, FL: Charisma House, 2014.

Bolz, Shawn. *Translating God*. Self-published, 2015.

Brown, Michael L. *Let No One Deceive You*. Shippensburg, PA: Destiny Image, 1997.

Chavda, Mahesh. *Only Love Can Make a Miracle*. Self-published, 2002.

Chavda, Mahesh and Bonnie Chavda. *Watch of the Lord*. Lake Mary, FL: Charisma House, 1999.

Frangipane, Francis. *Discerning of Spirits*. Cedar Rapids, IA: Arrow Publications, 1994.

———. *The Three Battlegrounds*. Cedar Rapids, IA: Arrow Publications, 2006.

Hamon, Jane. *Dreams and Visions*, rev. ed. Bloomington, MN: Chosen Books, 2016.

Hotchkin, Robert. *Leviathan Exposed*. Maricopa, AZ: XP Publishing, 2016.

Jacobs, Cindy. *Deliver Us from Evil*. Ventura, CA: Regal Books [Gospel Light], 2010.

———. *The Voice of God* rev. ed. Bloomington, MN: Chosen Books, 2016.

Johnson, Bill. *God Is Good*. Shippensburg, PA: Destiny Image, 2016.

———. *The Supernatural Power of a Transformed Mind*, rev. ed. Shippensburg, PA: Destiny Image, 2014.

Joyner, Rick. *Overcoming Evil in the Last Days*, rev. ed. with study guide. Shippensburg, PA: Destiny Image, 2009.

———. *The Prophetic Ministry*. Fort Mill, SC: MorningStar Publications, 2006.

King, Patricia. *Eyes That See*, rev. ed. Maricopa, AZ: XP Publishing, 2010.

———. *Developing Your Five Spiritual Senses*. Maricopa, AZ: XP Publishing, 2014.

LeClaire, Jennifer. *The Spiritual Warrior's Guide to Defeating Jezebel*. Bloomington, MN: Chosen Books, 2013.

Malick, Faisal. *The Political Spirit*. Shippensburg, PA: Destiny Image, 2008.

Maloney, James. *The Panoramic Seer*. Shippensburg, PA: Destiny Image, 2012.

Nelson, Jerame. *Activating Your Spiritual Senses*. Self-published through Living at His Feet Publications, San Diego, CA, 2012.

Pierce, Chuck D. *Time to Defeat the Devil*. Lake Mary, FL: Charisma House, 2011.

———. *A Time to Triumph*. Bloomington, MN: Chosen Books, 2016.

Prince, Derek. *Blessing or Curse: You Can Choose*. Bloomington, MN: Chosen Books, 2006.

——. *They Shall Expel Demons*. Bloomington, MN: Chosen Books, 1998.

Robinson, Mickey. *The Prophetic Made Personal*. Shippensburg, PA: Destiny Image, 2010.

Sandford, John and Paula Sandford. *The Elijah Task*. Lake Mary, FL: Charisma House, 2006.

Sheets, Dutch. *Intercessory Prayer*. Bloomington, MN: Bethany House, 1996 [reprint edition 2016].

Smith, Laura Harris. *Seeing the Voice of God*. Bloomington, MN: Chosen Books, 2014.

Virkler, Mark and Patti Virkler. *Communion with God – Study Guide*. Shippensburg, PA: Destiny Image, 1991.

Wagner, C. Peter. *Freedom from the Religious Spirit*. Ventura, CA: Regal Books [Gospel Light], 2005.

Wagner, Doris M. *How to Cast Out Demons*. Ventura, CA: Renew Books [Gospel Light], 2000.

Welton, Jonathan. *The School of Seers*, rev. ed. Shippensburg, PA: Destiny Image, 2013.

Wimber, John and Kevin Springer. *Power Healing*. New York: HarperOne, 2009.

ADDITIONAL RESOURCES BY JAMES W. GOLL

*(Many titles feature a matching study guide,
as well as audio and video presentations.)*

Adventures in the Prophetic (with Michal Ann Goll, Mickey Robinson, Patricia King, Jeff Jansen, and Ryan Wyatt)

Angelic Encounters (with Michal Ann Goll)

The Call to the Elijah Revolution (with Lou Engle)

The Coming Israel Awakening

Deliverance from Darkness

Dream Language (with Michal Ann Goll)

Exploring Your Dreams and Visions

Finding Hope

God Encounters Today (with Michal Ann Goll)

Hearing God's Voice Today

The Lifestyle of a Prophet

The Lifestyle of a Watchman

The Lost Art of Intercession

The Lost Art of Practicing His Presence

The Lost Art of Pure Worship (with Chris Dupré and contributions from Jeff Deyo, Sean Feucht, Julie Meyer, and Rachel Goll Tucker)

Living a Supernatural Life

Passionate Pursuit

Prayer Storm

Praying for Israel's Destiny

The Prophetic Intercessor

A Radical Faith

Releasing Spiritual Gifts Today

The Seer

Shifting Shadows of Supernatural Experiences (with Julia Loren)

Women on the Frontlines series: *A Call to Compassion, A Call to Courage,* and *A Call to the Secret Place* (Michal Ann Goll with James W. Goll)

ABOUT THE AUTHOR

James W. Goll is the founder of God Encounters Ministries. He is also the founder of Prayer Storm and the Worship City Alliance, as well as cofounder of Women on the Frontlines and Compassion Acts. James is a member of the Harvest International Ministries Apostolic Team and the Apostolic Council of Prophetic Elders. He serves as a core instructor in the Wagner Leadership Institute.

After pastoring in the Midwest United States, James was thrust into the role of an international equipper and trainer. He has traveled to over fifty nations, carrying a passion for Jesus wherever he goes. His desire is to see the body of Christ become the house of prayer for all nations and be empowered by the Holy Spirit to spread the Good News of Jesus to every country and to all peoples.

James and Michal Ann Goll were married for thirty-two years before her graduation to heaven in the fall of 2008. James has four wonderful adult children and a growing number of grandchildren. He makes his home amid the southern hills of Franklin, Tennessee.

For more information:

James W. Goll
God Encounters Ministries
P.O. Box 1653
Franklin, TN 37065
Phone: 1–877–200–1604

Websites:
www.godencounters.com ✦ www.jamesgoll.com

E-mail:
info@godencounters.com ✦ invitejames@godencounters.com

Social Media:
Follow James on
Facebook, Instagram, Twitter, XPMedia, GEM Media, Kingdom
Flame, YouTube, Vimeo, Charisma Blog, and iTunes

Free Inspiring Messages

 Video |  Audio |  Blog

Did you know that we have hundreds of free teaching articles, as well as audio and video messages for you to stream or download?

We believe they will revitalize you and give you hope.

It's amazing how far a little inspiration, encouragement and even challenge can go to help you break through old ruts and places of stagnancy in your spiritual life.

Stir up the fire in your spiritual life today!

GOD ENCOUNTERS MINISTRIES
with James W. Goll

Go to
www.GodEncounters.com